BEL CANTO
PRINCIPLES AND PRACTICES
By Cornelius L. Reid

Titles by the same Author

VOICE: PSYCHE AND SOMA

THE FREE VOICE: A GUIDE TO NATURAL SINGING

A DICTIONARY OF VOCAL TERMINOLOGY: AN ANALYSIS

BEL CANTO
PRINCIPLES AND PRACTICES
By Cornelius L. Reid

NEW YORK

Second Printing, 1974
Third Printing, 1978
Fourth Printing, 1984
Fifth Printing, 1990
Digital Printing, 2024

Library of Congress Cataloging-in-Publication Data

Names: Reid, Cornelius L.

Title: BEL CANTO Principles and Practices / Cornelius L. Reid.

Description: New Digital Printing | New York, NY | 2024

Includes bibliographical references

ISBN: paperback ISBN 979-8-9866347-2-2

Subjects: LCSH: Singing--Instruction and study.

Classification: ICC MT820 .R365 2018 | DDC 783/.043--dc23

International Standard Book Number: 979-8-9866347-2-2
Library of Congress Catalogue Number: 76-368704

Republished 1972, by The Joseph Patelson Music House
Printed in the United States of America

Digitally Published 2024

There are a hundred requisites necessary to constitute a good singer, of which one gifted with a fine voice is already in possession of ninety-nine.

OLD PROVERB

PREFACE

The theories contained in the following analysis of Bel Canto are wholeheartedly subscribed to by the author, and form the basis of his own teaching practices. The principles of tone production put forward as being the foundation upon which all good singing rests, however, did not originate with him, but represent what experience has demonstrated to be the sum and substance of enlightened practical and theoretical opinion.

The authorities quoted throughout this book have all been eminent in the profession, many as outstanding performers, all as teachers and theoreticians whose work in building great voices has been without parallel in the history of singing.

Most of the information contained herein is subject matter to which students today have difficulty of access, having neither the time, patience, nor experience in their student days to search in somewhat inaccessible places to acquire the information they so urgently need. It is the writer's sincere hope that the material here presented will fill this gap.

C. L. R.

Acknowledgments

The selection from Lilli Lehmann: *How to Sing*, translated by Richard Aldrich, copyright 1902, 1914, and 1924, used with the permission of The Macmillan Company.

The excerpts from Salvatore Marchesi: *A Vademecum for Singing Teachers and Pupils*, copyright 1902 by G. Schirmer, Inc., reprinted by permission.

TABLE OF CONTENTS

INTRODUCTION

Today, more than three hundred years after the invention of opera and the inception of the greatest era of virtuoso singing in the history of music, the need is more urgent than ever before to return to those principles of vocal technique responsible for that era of greatness.

In the century preceding our own, and more especially the seventeenth and eighteenth centuries, the art of Bel Canto singing had a very real meaning, both as to the style itself and with regard to the basic principles of tone production resulting in that style. Very definite rules governed the procedures adopted to train the voice, and, because these rules were in agreement with Nature's laws, the progress of every student was not only assured but occurred at a rate commensurate with his talent.

Very little is now known of the actual fundamentals of Bel Canto as they were applied during the seventeenth and eighteenth centuries. Because of the increasing diversity of modern 'methods' and a marked tendency to give greater prominence to the role played by the method itself than to the result of that method, a practice inevitably leading to bad singing, it is important that teachers of singing once again turn to authoritative sources for guidance and enlightenment. With the failure of modern methods of voice training being demonstrated in the city auditoriums year after year, the time is now ripe for the restoration of those principles of Bel Canto practiced with such unqualified success so long ago.

One of the sadder commentaries on our musical present is the obvious fact that *use* of the voice invariably means *abuse*. Few are the singers who survive the instruction to which they have been subjected, and it is a great rarity for any singer approaching the age of fifty to retain the freshness and vitality of tone production natural to all well-used voices. Premature vocal deterioration is entirely due to faulty technique, as a singer's vocal powers should remain unimpaired until he suffers a noticeable decline in health.

Some indication of the extent to which use of the voice has become synonymous with abuse may be had by reading the reviews appearing in the daily papers covering recital appearances or operatic performances of both new and familiar singers. *Seldom*, from the standpoint of pure vocal technique, does one read of firm, freely produced, enjoyable voices. *Almost never*, in the case of annual recitals, is the reviewer able to state that the vocalist has improved, except in poise and musicianship, with the passing years. Those who are able to maintain a place in the profession usually do so because their innate musicianship rises above the unfortunate limitations prescribed by a gradually retrogressing vocal technique. Formerly, when the basic principles of Bel Canto were commonly known and applied, premature vocal deterioration was almost unheard of.

The reason for present-day vocal deterioration will be shown to be faulty teaching. In most instances basic principles of tone production have been discarded, and supplanted by ill-defined concepts almost wholly without factual basis, such as 'voice placement,' 'nasal resonance,' 'breath control' and 'singing on the breath.' *Symptoms* of correct singing have been given credit for being direct causes of correct singing, with the result that almost all instruction has been removed from a concrete, factual basis to one that is, at best, weak, tentative and illusory.

Recent developments in modern instruction have featured the entry of the scientific investigator into the field of vocal technique. Rather than having clarified the already confused status of voice-training procedures, however, the vocal scientists, even the most reputable, have been in sharp disagreement on the most fundamental issues and as yet have contributed little to advance the art of singing.

Out of this background it is difficult, if not impossible, for the modern student to acquire a durable and efficient vocal technique. Faced with a diversity of methods that are contradictory to the extreme, the student today is too often confronted with the task of searching vainly for help and guidance.

The extent to which contemporary teaching methods have abandoned genuine principles of tone production for highly questionable procedures is best illustrated by an episode recently told the writer by a reputable concert and opera singer. Once, while filling an engagement to sing the Verdi *Requiem*, this artist witnessed a most extraordinary incident. Shortly before the performance was to begin, the contralto soloist, an artist-pupil attending one of the leading conservatories in the East, asked permission of the others to vocalize. Taking a small piece of bread from her purse the contralto placed it in her mouth, chewed gently and then proceeded to sing various musical figures on 'mee,' 'moo,' 'moh,' etc. When asked the purpose of this strange deportment, she replied in all seriousness, 'It relaxes the jaw and frees the tone'!

Jaw tension, of course, is one of the common difficulties with which students of singing have to contend. However, jaw tension is caused by a faulty technique of singing and is a condition that can only be corrected or alleviated by applying the first principles of tone production, namely, purity of vowel quality within a properly balanced registration. All efforts to obtain a relaxed jaw must end in failure unless the *cause* of jaw tension is first removed. As jaw tension is brought about by either throatiness or an unbalanced registration this condition cannot be corrected by chewing on a piece of bread, or by 'bringing the tone forward,' but by closely applying the first principles of Bel Canto instruction by means of which the technique is altered, causing the jaw tension to release.

So many quack remedies similar to the bread-chewing episode are now extant that one may readily discern why it is difficult, if not impossible, for the modern student of singing to master a sound technique of tone production. Most of the material now used as standard teaching guides displays wrong thinking and forms illogical conclusions. Because they have been taught to *think wrongly* in terms of tone production, singers today are not only unable to develop their latent talent and abilities but often find their careers prematurely curtailed because of voice failure.

In seeking to find a solution to present-day problems of voice training, therefore, it is the aim of this work to attempt to revitalize the basic principles of tone production employed by the teachers who were responsible for the Bel Canto style of singing. This vocal style produced a great 'Golden Age of Song.' Investigation will reveal that this was no accident, but the result of a system of vocalization whose principles were in direct conformity with Nature's laws. Examination of the historic background of Bel Canto and the writings of those who were most prominent as teachers of voice will prove conclusively that it was skill in the development of the voice, and not mere chance, that was responsible for this era of greatness.

CHAPTER I

HISTORIC BACKGROUND OF BEL CANTO

The Golden Age Of Song flourished in Italy during the post-Renaissance period. Before that time great voices and fine singing had been no novelty, but with the invention of opera in 1601 a more spectacular outlet was provided for vocal display and the virtuosity of the singers made more apparent. No longer were vocalists obliged to submit to the rigid discipline of the polyphonic style, and with the removal of many of the restrictions necessarily imposed by that style a new era began.

Many fabulous reputations for vocal perfection were built during the formative years of opera, and to a considerable extent the skill of the vocalists may be traced to the fundamental soundness of the basic principles used in developing their voices. Because of the confusion created by the contradictions and diversity of method common to present-day teaching practices, it is imperative at this time to restate and re-examine those basic principles of tone production used so successfully in establishing what is now known as the Bel Canto tradition.

The place occupied by the Golden Age of Song in the pages of musical history is due to an expansion of opportunity rather than newly discovered techniques of tone production. The church, heretofore the principal sponsor of the professional singer, was strongly opposed to all vocal display and made no allowance for the whims of the virtuoso. The wordly atmosphere of the theater, however, did provide an environment suitable for virtuoso performance and into these new surroundings the vocally proficient fitted admirably.

A brief examination of the facts concerning the early development of opera will help clarify the relationship of the singing virtuoso to the new art form, and show the underlying reasons for the pre-eminence of the vocalist at that particular time.

The lyric drama, as it is known today, is the outgrowth of an attempt on the part of a select circle of intellectuals to recreate the stage traditions of the ancient Greeks. The Florentine aristocrat, Count Bardi, was one of the most enthusiastic supporters of this movement and every facility of his elaborate household was given over to forwarding the plans jointly agreed upon.

Among those attracted to the congenial atmosphere of the Bardi establishment were such outstanding personalities as Caccini, Strozzi, Mei, Corsi, Vincenzo Galilei, Peri and Rinuccini. The first experiment of the *Camerata*, as this group called itself, was a setting of the legend of *Daphne and Apollo*. The poet Ottavio Rinuccini prepared a libretto, and Jacopo Peri collaborated with Giulio Caccini in composing the musical score. It was at this particular moment that the leadership of the *Camerata* passed from Count Bardi to Jacopo Corsi, so it was in the latter's home, *circa* 1594, that the performance was given.

While the initial experiment with *Daphne* was probably never intended to provide more than a pleasant evening's entertainment for the friends of the *Camerata*, so enthusiastic was the response of the audience that a second venture was planned by the producers. Rinuccini adapted another Greek tragedy, *Euridice*, while Peri and Caccini again joined forces to compose the music. This novelty was planned and staged for the celebration of the marriage of Henry IV of France to Maria de' Medici, and was first performed at Florence in the year 1600.

Up to this time the development of music for the voice had largely centered upon polyphonic writing, which had been brought to a high level of perfection. As far as its adaptability to the purposes of the stage was concerned, however, the polyphonic style was of exceedingly dubious value. The very nature of its structural form, where each part is independent yet absolutely interdependent, made no allowance for dramatic action. Stage business quickly destroyed the finely interwoven harmonic unit, which in turn could only be preserved by restricting the freedom of movement so necessary to effective drama. Polyphony tended to contain all motion within narrowly circumscribed limits and was, therefore, unsuitable for adaptation to the lyric stage.

With these considerations in mind the *Camerata* determined to alter the style of choral writing and subordinate all ensemble to its proper place in the dramatic action. Individuals were selected to portray the *dramatis personae*. This having been done, it was immediately apparent that numerous impediments to the logical unfolding of the drama had been removed. Those who had been selected to represent a character of the play were given a melody to sing. By means of these melodies they expressed in solo form the hopes, feelings, aspirations and frustrations ascribed to that individual. In this way *monody*, or the lyric solo, was brought into use.

After the monodic form of composition had become well established even greater freedom was afforded by separating the melody into two parts: first, the *aria*; second, a quasi song-speech called *recitative*. Under this arrangement the details and lesser incidents of the story were carried rapidly forward by the recitative to those moments of greatest emotional impact. The climactic points of the drama were then expressed in the aria, or by an ensemble of solo voices ranging in size from a duo to a sextet, according to the dramatic situation.

For almost half a century the proponents of the new music steadfastly pursued their artistic ideals. Drama, music, décor and action were skillfully blended together making *opera*, as it was called, one of the great arts.

Public enthusiasm for the new art form may be judged by the rapidity with which new theaters devoted to operatic performances sprang into being. Before the close of the century more than twenty houses were prospering in the larger Italian cities. Six hundred and fifty-eight music dramas were composed during this period, one hundred being performed between 1662 and 1680 alone. However, it was not entirely the spectacular and novel music drama that attracted the interest of the people. The dazzling vocal feats of the leading singers who dominated every performance astonished and delighted audiences everywhere and the demand for opera continued to grow. Pampered and celebrated, the singer had become the lion of the hour.

One of the earliest developments in monody was the introduction of the *da capo* aria. This is a simple three-part song form where the third section is a restatement, or repetition, of the first, as A-B-A. During this time it became customary in the performance of the *da capo* aria to allow the singer a certain freedom from the strict observance of the written notation. The first part of the aria was traditionally sung as the composer had indicated. With the repeat of the first section, however, it soon became mandatory for the vocalist to interpolate his own embellishments in order to display the fullest extent of the vocal resources at his command, as well as exhibit his musical taste in improvisation.

The ability to improvise was called by the early Italians, *cantar al mente*, and was considered to be the highest refinement of the singer's art. Classical musicians, whether instrumentalists or vocalists, no longer follow this custom, but its counterpart may be found in modern jazz when the performer 'takes off,' or 'rides' an *ad libitum* chorus. Over a groundwork of basic harmonies that remain unchanged in the accompaniment, the jazz soloist, like his vocal predecessor, is free to introduce any thematic variation he chooses. To select embellishments with taste and an understanding of style demands of the performer a security of technique and a superiority of musicianship that has become very rare.

What at first amounted to discreet liberty in the matter of performing *ad libitum*, however, soon degenerated into license. Freedom to extemporize on a musical theme presented the singing virtuosi of the time with an opportunity for vocal display too tempting to be resisted. In the mad scramble for public favor that naturally followed, the ideals of the *Camerata* were hastily abandoned. The vocal virtuoso had come into his own.

Just how completely all sense of proportion was lost by singers, composers, audience and all concerned in the performance of opera, may be judged from a comment by Benedetto Marcello published in a famous pamphlet called *Il Teatro Alla Moda*, The Theatre in High Style (Venice, 1721). Of the habits of the singers he relates: 'Singing the aria, he may well decide that he will pause where and when he pleases; in the cadenzas improvising such passages and embellishments that the orchestra director lifts his hands from the harpsichord and takes a pinch of snuff while he awaits the pleasure of the *divo*. He will treat the dramatic action according to his own caprice, since the modern artist need not understand the sentiments expressed in his own words, nor trouble himself to co-operate by gestures or movements. Singing the *da capo* he will change the whole aria to suit himself, even though his changes have no connection whatever with the harmony of the author, or the convenience of the orchestra players, and though these variations may even include a change of tempo. No one cares, since the composer of the music is resigned to anything.'

With the audience showing considerably greater interest in the vocal display dominating every performance than in the drama or the music itself, all consideration of art was quickly forgotten. With the ever increasing extravagance of the singing virtuosi, opera retrogressed to the extent of becoming an endless cycle of roulades, trills, cadenzas, and embellishments of one kind or another. Unity was sacrificed for display, and all melodies made to sound like endless scale passages.

Finally the composers themselves bowed to popular demand and the willfulness of the vocalists and wrote highly ornamental pieces completely lacking in substance and musical worth. Opera, consequently, degenerated into a set pattern of concert pieces designed to exhibit the vocal powers and prowess of the great voices of the day. However, while opera as an art form was in a state of decadence, this period of musical history became known as the 'Golden Age of Song.' During this era the art of singing is acknowledged to have achieved its highest perfection. The vocal style became known as 'Bel Canto,' or beautiful singing.

Inasmuch as the precise nature of the vocal instruction of this period has been lost as it passed through succeeding generations, this age contains considerably more than historical interest. It was a time of wonderfully compelling voices of great limpidity, extremely wide range, amazing flexibility and beautiful quality. The impetus gained by the full flowering of the vocal art in Italy not only caused the fame of the Bel Canto style of singing to spread over the entire continent of Europe but established principles of vocal technique that affected, to a gradually lessening degree, the vocal art of the eighteenth, nineteenth and twentieth centuries as well.

Should any doubt be entertained as to the extraordinary vocal powers of the singers of the Bel Canto era, the following excerpt from Bontempi's *Historica Musica* should satisfy even the most cynical. Commenting on the performance of Baldassare Ferri (1610-1680), he maintains, 'One who has not heard this sublime singer can form no idea of the limpidity of his voice, of his agility, of his marvelous facility in the most difficult passages, of the justness of his intonation, the brilliancy of his trill, of his inexhaustible respiration. One often heard him perform rapid and difficult passages with every shade of crescendo and diminuendo. Then, when it seemed as if he ought to be tired, he would launch on his interminable trill and mount and descend on it all the degrees of the chromatic scale through a range of two octaves with unerring justice. And all this was but play for him.'

When these accomplishments are measured against those possessed by singers appearing before the public today, some idea of the advantages of mastering the art of Bel Canto singing may be gained. Few singers today can sing two octaves comfortably, much less trill on all the degrees of the chromatic scale. Such vocalization is, indeed, unusual, but unusual vocalization was almost commonplace to those thoroughly schooled in the technique of Bel Canto. The singing of Farinelli, Senesino, Crescentini, Cafferelli, and many others too numerous to mention, was reputedly of the same style and accomplishment.

Although all of these singers mentioned were among the *castrati* enjoying such a vogue at that time, it would be a serious mistake to imagine that extraordinary singing was the exclusive province of the male soprano. Pietro della Valle, in a letter addressed to Lelio Guidicioni in 1640, enthused over the superb singing of the Nuns of Santa Lucia, San Silvestro, Magnanopolis, and Santa Chiara. Caccini's daughter and, later, Cuzzoni, Faustina Bordoni and Lucrezia Agujari were included among the professional vocalists whose technique paralleled that of the *evirati* in every respect.

As a general rule voices having a high *tessitura* were greatly preferred to lower voices and the operatic hero and heroine were always the tenor and soprano. The basic principles of Bel Canto, however, arc equally applicable and no less beneficial to all voices. Boschi and Montanagna, two great Handelian bassos, possessed a vocal facility comparable in every way to that of the lighter voices and matched their technical accomplishments in every detail. To overlook the fact that basses and contraltos were equally gifted, vocally, as the sopranos would be to underestimate seriously the soundness of the vocal instruction available to them.

An Italian writer, Arteaga, in an article appearing in *Le Revoluzione del Teatro Musicale Italiano* (Venice, 1785) very ably sums up the musical situation of the Bel Canto era when he wrote, 'But nothing contributes so much to clarify Italian music at that time as the excellence and abundance of the singers.'

AN EXAMPLE OF EARLY COLORATURA - Passages sung by Lucrezia Agujari in the presence of Mozart at Parma during his Italian tour in 1770. Agujari was one of the fabulous vocalists of the Bel Canto era. Mozart described her voice as 'lovely, and of unbelievable range.'

CHAPTER II

EARLY HISTORY OF VOICE TRAINING

The Bel Canto style of singing, or the principles of tone production resulting in that style, did not originate with the invention of opera. Hundreds of years had already been spent perfecting techniques and discovering the innermost secrets of the art. The final perfection of the style was an outgrowth of a long evolutionary process whose origins are lost in antiquity.

Systematic instruction in the art of singing is known to have been established as early as the fourth century, when canons, i.e., singers, were ordained into the church to perform the musical service. Just as the great sculptors, painters and architects were employed to beautify the edifice where people worshipped, so music was developed for the purpose of glorifying God. This sense of dedication was so strong in the minds of the clergy that in 350 a.d. the Laodicean Council, and later the Fourth Council of Carthage, decreed in effect that congregational singing interfered with the beauty of the musical service. Rules of procedure were drawn up designed to govern and restrict the active participation of the people in the service of worship. All of the musical service but the hymn singing was decreed to be the exclusive province of a choir made up of highly trained singers.

During the fourth century the vocal development of both the clergy and members of the choir became the direct responsibility of the *Schola Cantorum*, a musical conservatory established by Pope Sylvester (314-336 a.d.). At this school instruction was provided in the basic principles of tone production and musical theory.

The status of the *Schola Cantorum*, however, remained somewhat unstable until 600 a.d. when Pope Gregory supported the work of the school by generously increasing its endowment and facilities. Two buildings near Lateran were set aside for its use. In one of these the singers and clergy lived together, while the other became an orphanage to which those who were talented were sent for musical instruction. There the student was set to the arduous task of becoming a musician and a vocal artist.

Some idea of the intense enthusiasm with which all concerned threw themselves into the work of the *Schola* may be had when it is realized that Pope Gregory found it necessary to warn the priests against devoting too much time to the problems of voice training to the neglect of their clerical duties.

As the term of apprenticeship at the *Schola Cantorum* covered a span of nine years it is quite evident that a very comprehensive course of study was undertaken, and that the musical preparation given these students was directed toward a thorough mastery over every phase of the vocal art. In the highest sense and meaning of the word these students became well-schooled singers and masters of a sound technique of tone production. Today, of course, even though students pursue their studies for an equivalent length of time, such accomplishment is highly exceptional rather than general.

Because of a complete absence of scientific knowledge upon subjects related to voice it was impossible for the early systems of training to be founded upon principles other than those growing out of empirical observation. Yet, in view of the extraordinary accomplishments of the vocalists trained by these procedures the instruction must have been securely based upon principles that were both scientifically sound and aesthetically satisfying.

A surprisingly complete record of the opinions of the early teachers of singing has been preserved and is contained in the writings of several men who in their own teaching represented the highest ideals and finest traditions of Bel Canto. One of the most important of these, Giulio Caccini, was a member of the *Camerata*.

Like so many musicians of the Renaissance period, Caccini was, together with being an excellent composer and instrumentalist, a famous singer and teacher of singing. With the publication of his book, *Nuove Musiche* (1601), he touched lightly upon some of the problems of voice training as it was understood and practiced in his time. These disclosures, however, suffer from a want of detailed analysis, and the principles of vocal technique brought under discussion were placed in a position subordinate to a subject evidently less well understood, namely, monody and the opera.

A much more important and comprehensive report on the principles of Bel Canto was left by Pietro Francesco Tosi in a book, *Observations on the Florid Song,* published in Bologna in 1723. Tosi, like Caccini, was a renowned singer and composer who later became one of the most celebrated singing masters of his time. He was fortunate in being the son of a famous musician and was without doubt well informed regarding the vocal practices and traditions of a generation preceding his own. As a performer his fame extended over the entire continent of Europe. His last years were spent teaching in England.

Half a century after the publication of Tosi's enlightening treatise another celebrated teacher of singing, Giovanni Battista Mancini, brought out a book called *Practical Reflections on the Figurative Art of Singing* (Milan, 1776). This book constitutes the most complete and authoritative source material that has ever been published on the subject of Bel Canto. Mancini was a direct lineal descendant of the Bel Canto tradition. As a pupil of Bernacchi he became one of the great singers of the eighteenth century. When he later became a teacher it is reasonable to assume that he retained intact those principles of vocal technique he had learned as a student.

The principles of Bel Canto and the singing technique that Mancini acquired from Bernacchi very likely were in keeping with those the latter had learned from his teacher, Pistocchi. This history is an interesting one. Pistocchi, after achieving a world-wide reputation as a singer, returned to Bologna and established a school of singing whose success made that city the center of Italian voice culture. When Bernacchi had the tragic misfortune in his youth to have had his voice seriously impaired by bad teaching methods he presented himself to Pistocchi and begged him to restore his voice. After three years of diligent study Bernacchi's voice responded so well that he was again able to take his place before the public and became known as one of the most accomplished and gifted singers of the age.

The case history of Bernacchi is doubly interesting because of the fact that there is now a tendency in some quarters to deprecate the accomplishments of the teachers of this period and to dismiss their achievements by asserting that they consented to teach only those who had naturally fine voices which required no more than superficial technical instruction. This attitude is difficult to understand. Did Porpora keep Cafferelli occupied with a single sheet of exercise material for six years because he was already a perfect singer? Hardly. By restoring Bernacchi's injured voice to perfect health Pistocchi convincingly demonstrated that the essence of Bel Canto is to be found in its positive, rather than negative, effect. Those principles of tone production applied in training the voice at that time not only worked toward its preservation but were sufficiently basic to restore a damaged organ to its fullest vitality.

As a teacher of singing Bernacchi was completely successful. In addition to Mancini he also taught such wonderful vocalists as Raff, Mengozzi and Carestini. Therefore, Mancini may be considered a legitimate heir to the most authentic and authoritative sources and traditions of Bel Canto.

With one or two noteworthy exceptions, almost all that is now known of Bel Canto is contained in the writings of these three teachers, and it is interesting to note that they are almost unanimous in their support of every fundamental principle of tone production. On virtually every important detail of vocal instruction they unite in wholehearted agreement, the later works merely amplifying those of earlier publication.

Quotations from other sources somewhat less authentic, but sufficiently authoritative, will be found to substantiate the validity and accuracy of the experience of these earlier writers.

CHAPTER III

THE BEL CANTO IDEAL

In order that the correctness of any training procedure may be accurately estimated and its value determined, it it essential for every teacher and student of singing to have an exact knowledge of the mechanical capacities and limitations of the human voice. An ideal vocal technique must be envisioned and this technique should become the goal toward which all the student's energies are to be directed.

Before entering into a discussion of the actual techniques used in developing the Bel Canto style of singing, therefore, it will be more advantageous to reflect for a moment on the full significance of the term 'Bel Canto' itself. By so doing, all qualities of tone will be found to be firmly rooted in the tangible rather than the intangible; and that tone quality always reflects the degree of efficiency with which the vocal mechanism is responding at a given time.

Translated, 'Bel Canto' may be interpreted to mean 'Beautiful Singing.' Accepted at face value, this expression is exceedingly vague and indefinite until it is realized that beautiful singing implies much more than an ability to produce lovely sounds. When a tone is truly beautiful it signifies that the vocal mechanism is functioning correctly, and that a complete harmony exists between aesthetic principles and those laws of Nature by which the operation of the vocal mechanism is governed. Bel Canto singing is impossible without vocal freedom, and true vocal freedom finds its expression in vitally resonant tones covering a wide pitch range, in a complete control over extremes of dynamics, and in ease and flexibility of execution. These characteristics of the perfectly used voice constitute the Bel Canto ideal, and are elements without which it would be impossible to have genuinely beautiful tone. In sacrificing every other consideration in the interest of tonal beauty the early Italian teachers instituted a sound basis for developing the voice.

With so great a dependency placed upon what at first appears to be solely an aesthetic principle one of the first problems of voice training is to reconcile concepts of beauty growing out of taste, experience and prejudice, and to bring them into agreement with Nature's laws.

The mistake to be avoided in estimating the purely technical merits of a vocalist's performance is to confuse such elements as personality and superior musicianship with sheer technical ability and to falsely attribute these virtues to skill in tone production. Although it must be acknowledged that a magnetic personality and sensitive musicianship are of inestimable value to the artist, these gifts must never be permitted to bias the judgment in purely technical matters. As the resourcefulness of the singer is so largely dependent upon the state of his technical proficiency, and the durability of his voice and the longevity of his career so wholly reliant upon having acquired a secure vocal technique, this technical phase of singing must be evaluated separately and judged independently on its own merits.

In learning to arrive at a correct estimate of a performer's technique, therefore, all considerations contributing to entertainment value, or even to art itself, must be carefully separated from the singer's mere physical skill in producing sound. After this has been done it becomes a relatively simple matter to arrive at an accurate estimate of the soundness of the voice production and correctly judge the relative degree of *natural* voice quality that is being revealed.

To establish a sound basis for determining the accuracy of an opinion relative to tonal beauty, therefore, it is not enough to merely listen to the quality of the tones being produced but it is also necessary to observe the mechanical response of the vocal organs. When it is apparent that difficulties are overcome with ease and sureness, the voice is not only being well produced but, *because it is well produced*, the quality must be relatively pure. Perfect tone qualities find their equivalent expression in complete vocal freedom. Conversely, inferior or imperfect qualities are always limited by restrictions which are in direct proportion to the degree of imperfection. A truly beautiful tone has few limitations and, because the operation of the vocal organs is in strict conformity with Nature, genuine feelings are aroused which are admirably adaptable to the purposes of artistic expression. Therefore, a beautiful tone must be considered a factual condition and not a matter of personal opinion.

While a discussion of the mysteries of the aesthetics of tone production often leads nowhere, the meaning of vocal freedom is self-evident. In the final analysis, vocal freedom, or that condition of the vocal organs which alone reveals the natural *timbre* of the voice, is simply a feeling of being able to sing higher and lower, louder and softer, with ease and comfort. In a physical sense this feeling of freedom indicates that the muscular co-ordination of the vocal mechanism has been brought into, or is already in, proper balance. Once concepts of quality have been brought into agreement with the organic laws by which the vocal organs are regulated, the voice acquires resonance, an extensive range, and flexibility. This condition shows an absence of resistance, or muscular interference, and is true vocal freedom.

The vocal organs, therefore, must be understood to have specific capacities and limitations, and in this sense the early Italian teachers considered the vocal organs, like any other mechanism producing tone, to be an instrument. All voice types were believed to meet a uniform standard of scale contour and dynamics. Every voice, under favorable technical conditions, was known to be able to produce resonant tones over a wide pitch range as well as possess the ability to swell and diminish fluently. Power and resonance was a definite factor, and a smooth, even transition from one extreme of range and intensity to its opposite indicated that the balance and co-ordination within the vocal mechanism were in correct adjustment. Only after these conditions had been successfully met was the quality of a singer's voice considered truly beautiful.

There are, it is true, many differences in quality exhibited by singers, but these are natural only so long as they do not appear as vocal limitations. Differences in quality may only be attributed to the general physical construction of the individual, to native temperament, natural *tessitura*, and vowel 'coloring' for purposes of artistic expression. Never, except in the rare instance of an actual physical impairment, is it admissible to acknowledge irregularities as being natural to the voice.

Typical examples of faulty technique which have more and more come to be accepted as 'natural' tone qualities may be heard in the voice of the average 'mezzo-soprano' or 'bass-baritone.' As it is not always discreet for teachers to confess an inability to set up correct conditions of tone production which alone can reveal the natural *timbre* and *tessitura* of the student's voice, it has become an increasingly common practice to establish new categories to describe the faults. Thus, voices that cannot sing high enough to be a soprano or low enough to be a contralto are called 'mezzo-sopranos.' However, the only genuine 'mezzo-soprano' voice is one which possesses a 'dark,' mellow quality of velvety richness, and whose comfortable voice range extends from a low B flat that is full and solid to a clear, ringing high C. The so-called 'mezzo-soprano' who cannot do this merely has a 'thick,' artificial quality of little utility and less beauty.

Like the 'mezzo,' the 'bass-baritone' is rarely a genuine voice type, but also a voice of 'thick,' imposed quality lacking both the high tones of the real baritone and the low tones of the true basso. Proper training procedure invariably rectifies this condition and the voice readily seeks that *tessitura* to which it belongs.

Other offenders in this regard are the 'lyric-tenors' who are unable to sing low tones effectively. If the principles of Bel Canto were to be applied in developing the voices of all those who now consider themselves to be 'mezzos,' 'bass-baritones' and 'lyric- tenors,' very few singers would discover that their voices rightfully belonged in any of these categories. 'mezzos,' 'bass-baritones' and 'lyric-tenors' are rare, not commonplace, voice types.

It is important to realize, therefore, that qualities of sound growing out of vocal faults should never determine a 'type' of voice, and as long as qualities of this kind are accepted as legitimate almost no improvement can be expected of the singer. Vocal defects should be transitory, as they are due to an incorrect method of singing. The real cause of faulty emission lies with the tone quality itself, which must be altered and changed before any appreciable progress can be made toward vocal freedom. To remain satisfied with any quality that fails to provide the utmost vocal freedom with regard to power, wide range, and flexibility is to perpetuate one of the chief causes of faulty tone production.

Before making an effort to determine what is desirable and undesirable, essential and non-essential to the voice-building process, it is important that a clear understanding be had of those elements without which it would be impossible to have vocal tone. With this knowledge at hand it becomes easier to comprehend why the voice, when it is being correctly used, has a uniform outline of scale contour and dynamics.

The vocal organs produce sound, like the piano or violin, because an actuating force, or pressure, has been brought against a vibrator. With the piano it is the hammer striking against the string; with the violin it is the bow drawn across the strings; with the voice it is the pressure of the breath against the vocal cords that causes vibrations whose speed determines pitch.

Once the actuating force has set up vibrations, the chambers of resonance amplify the initial sounds produced by the vibrator so that the performer, by varying the pressure, is able to command a variety of intensities suitable to his artistic purpose. These intensities range, under suitable conditions of acoustics, from very soft to very loud.

Whichever instrument is brought under consideration, the guiding principles governing and determining the performer's skill remain unchanged. The one who has the correct technique of drawing sounds from the instrument is he who has learned to exploit and control the entire dynamic resources possessed by that instrument. The singer or player who can execute musical phrases at extreme degrees of intensity with perfect smoothness and evenness has acquired a solid and secure foundation of tone production, i.e., technique, and therefore will never have difficulty producing tones of medium loudness. Mastery over the extremes of intensity demands a perfection of muscular co-ordination which from the beginning of training should be the purpose and aim of all instruction. Only when the fullest acoustical resources of the instrument have been successfully exploited will the purest quality and fullest resonance be achieved.

The realization that the vocal organs form an instrument having potentialities of a specific nature, like all musical instruments, removes many misconceptions regarding 'natural' limitations. The only 'natural' limitations that should be recognized are those of technique, provided, of course, that the vocal organs are in a healthy condition and undamaged.

Faulty muscular co-ordination is almost always responsible for the failure of a singer to perform freely and tirelessly throughout the entire range of the voice at all intensities.

When a singer undertakes to learn a correct technique of voice production he is actually applying principles that will perfect the muscular co-ordination of the vocal mechanism. The success or failure of his effort can only be accurately measured by the way in which the voice responds. When the compass and range are gradually extended to include two and a half to three octaves, and the ability to swell and diminish fluently acquired, then the muscular organization has been effectively co-ordinated and the voice is being correctly used.

An analogy that is helpful in illustrating this fact is provided by two violinists, one an artist having great technical facility, the other an inexpert beginner. If the listener could hear each one play for a few minutes on the same Stradivarius what would the result be? The fine player, of course, would bring out beautiful, resonant tones that would be a revelation of the inherent musical capacities of the violin. The beginner, the inferior technician, would provide no such insight because of his inept handling of the instrument. From tones of exquisite beauty the quality of the violin would be changed immediately and become scratchy and ugly. All resonance latent within the instrument would lie dormant and no indication of its potentialities revealed. What is important to remember is that the latent capacity of the instrument remained unchanged in the hands of both players. The disparity in their playing was essentially a demonstration of dissimilar techniques. *The way the instrument was played* made all the difference.

It is this viewpoint of technique as applied to the voice that both teachers and students of singing must come to appreciate. There is only one way of singing freely in the high, low and intermediary ranges of the voice smoothly and easily, and that is the *correct* way. By the same reasoning, the singer who fails to acquire a technique permitting complete vocal freedom in matters of power, range and flexibility must have an incorrect way of singing.

The test of quality, therefore, is not alone made by judging the pleasing nature of the sounds produced, but by checking one's aesthetic judgment by measuring the capacities and capabilities of the quality *assumed* to be beautiful, against that of the ideal voice. Not all singers, it is true, possess voices of equal beauty, as the structure and conformation of the anatomical parts vary. But, other things being equal, every voice that is properly used should sound lovely and musical. However, when one singer can manage two and a half to three octaves with freedom and ease, while another is reduced to one and a half octaves, or barely two, the deficiency is seldom due to a permanent physical disability but is the result of faulty technique.

To a large extent the talent and ability of both student and teacher may be measured by the strength by which they are instinctively drawn to that which is truly beautiful. All aesthetic principles involved in singing are finally resolved when the tones selected for developing the voice are actually purer and, therefore, better produced. When the aesthetic judgment is correct the voice will immediately, if gradually, respond by a steady increase in power, resonance, range and flexibility. Thus, Bel Canto not only signifies that the tone is beautiful but that the fullest resources of the vocal mechanism have been utilized.

To show how successful the early teachers of Bel Canto were in developing the voice and helping to fulfill the promise of the students entrusted to their care, it is only necessary to review some of the critical comments made by qualified observers. It is interesting, but not surprising, to note the uniformity and similarity of the descriptions used in recording the abilities of the leading singers of that era.

A general discussion of the Bel Canto style is included in an article published in the *Mercure de France*, contributed by a writer who lived in Venice during the last years of the seventeenth century. An enthusiastic admirer of the new art form, and especially of the singing that was to be heard at the time, this writer comments that 'the voices are clear, pure, solid and bold, without pinching and constraint.'

Mancini, who represented the consensus of enlightened critics of his generation, once commented on the performance of Farinelli. 'His voice,' he records, 'was thought a marvel because it was so perfect, so powerful, so sonorous and so rich in its extent, both in the high and in the low parts of the register, that its equal has never been heard in our time. The qualities in which he excelled was in the evenness of his voice, the union of the registers, the art of swelling its sound, the portamento, a surprising agility, a graceful and pathetic style, and a shake as admirable as it was rare.' (33).*

Quantz, an eminent historian of music and court musician to Frederick the Great, wrote extravagant praise of the tone production of Carestini who, he claims, 'sang after the manner of Farinelli.'

A story is told in connection with Farinelli's singing, giving some idea as to the wonderful resonance of his voice. At one time while he was in Rome he became involved in a debate bearing upon the relative merits and expressive capacities of the voice and the trumpet. A contest was arranged with one of the leading trumpet virtuosi of the city, and one of the largest theaters engaged so that the public could witness the exhibition. The completed arrangements permitted each of the contestants several trials for the purpose of demonstrating his technical prowess and to serve as a basis of comparison in judging the extent of their abilities.

After each performer had given many brilliant examples of his skill, the singer was finally declared to be the winner. Not only did Farinelli

____

* Numbers in parentheses refer to the Bibliography

actually surpass the trumpet in the art of swelling and diminishing each tone, but showed that the voice is the more flexible instrument by excelling in coloratura passages and *bravura* effects. In addition, which is more surprising, he equalled the trumpet in power, clarity and brilliance.

As Farinelli was considered to be the perfect exponent of Bel Canto singing there can be no question but that power, i.e., resonance, or volume, was looked upon as a requisite to beautiful tone, together with purity of intonation, flexibility and an extensive vocal range. These factors combined are the result of a correct technique of tone production and constituted the Bel Canto ideal.

Additional insight into the singing style of the Bel Canto era is provided by Richard Mackenzie Bacon in *Elements of Vocal Science* (1824). Concerning the singing style of this period he writes, 'The very essence of Italian singing I take it to be, that it is *dramatic*.' This is an opinion shared by relatively few present-day teachers of singing, who are more inclined toward the belief that sweet, light-voiced singing more closely represents the Bel Canto ideal.

Bacon is even more explicit in his description of the Italian vocalists and goes on to say, 'Their conceptions are directed to objects of the most intense and vivid expression and hence it also follows that the means they use are of the boldest and most striking character. They not only endeavor to raise the strongest emotions in the auditor and the spectator (for we shall find they assail both senses), but they aim at seeming *to be* (as nearly as possible) the person they are supposed to be singing, and to identify themselves with all the passions by which that individual is represented as being influenced. To this grand end they are incited by a naturally ardent temperament.'

It is somewhat difficult to believe that dramatic singing in the grand manner was the true Bel Canto vocal style. Yet, from sources equally authoritative it may be learned that this style of singing was the rule rather than the exception, both in the formative years of opera as well as later periods. Dr. Charles Burney, the distinguished world traveler and recorder of musical history, wrote enthusiastically about the singing of Manzolli, another great artist of the Bel Canto school who sang during the eighteenth century. Burney relates that 'Manzolli's voice was the most powerful and voluminous that had ever been heard on the English stage since the time of Farinelli. His manner of singing was grand and full of dignity.' (6).

Senesino, another fabulous vocal technician of this era, had, according to contemporary accounts, 'a clear, penetrating, equal and flexible' voice. 'His intonation was pure and his trill perfect.'

As comments concerning more recent favorites, all of whom became legendary figures, are examined it will be seen that the qualities and characteristics of their singing answered the same description as that applied to their predecessors. Jenny Lind's voice was 'a soprano of great compass and power, not less remarkable for its sweetness and perfect purity of tone.' Rubini's voice was praised as 'strong, just and clear.' Lablache's as 'pure, powerful and flexible.' The great Alboni possessed a vocal technique that enabled her to sing tones which 'poured out sonorously without the slightest effort, with sparkling facility.'

Adelina Patti's career is one that in more modern times has matched the performers of the earlier Bel Canto period and followed in the great tradition. *Grove's Dictionary of Music and Musicians* states that this singer was looked upon as the sole inheritor of the title '*Diva*' which descended to her from Grisi and Catalani. So extraordinary were the vocal powers of this singer that she was able to undertake roles of the greatest diversity. Not only was she famed for her brilliant performances of coloratura roles such as Ophelia, in *Hamlet*; Lakmé, in the opera of the same name; Lucia, in *Lucia di Lammermoor*; but she also sang the title role in *Carmen*, and successfully created the role of Aida, in Verdi's opera of that name, at

Covent Garden, London, in 1876. Her first professional appearance was made at the age of twelve; her last at the age of seventy-two, at a benefit for her by then indigent colleagues, Madame Albani and Wilhelm Ganz. There are those who claim her singing was unimpaired and incomparable to the end.

Ideal conditions of vocalization and tone production of this kind are not, of course, likely to occur very often. Few are privileged to achieve perfection. But it is a goal toward which every teacher and student of singing should strive! Tosi was aware of the dangers inherent in an attitude of self-satisfaction. This is his advice: 'He who does not strive with all diligence to attain the highest place in his profession soon begins to descend to the second, and gradually becomes satisfied with the lowest grade.' On the other hand, one must realize that there is a time element involved in mastering the art of singing, and that progress is gradual. To force progress is to attempt to overcome difficulties the vocal organs are not yet conditioned to handle. Caccini warned against this when he said, 'Many evils arise from the fact that the performer has not made himself quite master of that which he wishes to sing.'

How many of our young singers today are too easily satisfied and rely on strength of personality to overcome obvious vocal deficiencies! They seldom master that which they desire to sing and, by closing their eyes to vocal shortcomings, have become satisfied with a position holding little promise for themselves or for the future of art. Every conceivable excuse is made toward self-deception so that the work necessary to becoming an artist may be avoided. Why was Patti able to sing professionally for almost sixty years? Simply because she had perfected her vocal technique and never allowed the *use* of her voice to become *abuse*.

More up-to-date information concerning the Bel Canto tradition is supplied by Herman Klein, a prominent music critic, a pupil and former assistant to Manuel Garcia, who quotes from a letter received from his friend Percy Betts describing the debut of Enrico Caruso at Covent Garden in 1902. The great tenor's voice is analyzed as follows: 'He had a delightful *mezza voce*, and he had neither the nasal quality nor the "bleat" which are the bane of so many of our compatriots. His voice is of that soft, velvety quality, which old opera-goers will associate with Fancelli, and still older men with Giulini. It is, in fact, a pure tenor voice of the old Italian type.' (25).

This statement is interesting for two reasons. First, because Mr. Betts stresses the 'soft, velvety timbre,' rather than dwell on the tremendous power for which this artist was noted, and second, because he traces this style of tone production back to the 'old Italian type' of Bel Canto. Like Patti, Caruso could sing lyric as well as dramatic roles with complete facility and assurance, and was as famous for his Des Grieux in *Manon* as he was for his Rhadames in *Aida*.

It comes as somewhat of a revelation to learn from authoritative sources that resonance and an opulent tone quality were looked upon as being indispensable to a Bel Canto technique. For many years the belief has been that light, sweet singing in the half voice was more in keeping with the traditions of the old school. Bond, and lyric tenors of similar attainment, has long been praised as having been an outstanding representative of Bel Canto. However, if Caruso approximated the Italian ideal of Bel Canto, which he did although he lacked the musical suavity which would have made it more apparent, Bonci could not begin to approach it. The two singers were direct opposites in their technique of tone production. Few of the qualities and characteristics of Bonci's singing answered the description used in eulogizing Farinelli's performance. Caruso's singing bore a very close resemblance to it. Caruso followed the great Bel Canto tradition. Bonci did not.

Continuing through the years into the second so-called 'Golden Age of Song,' there still is to be noted the factor of power, wide range and extreme flexibility in the performance of the leading artists. Tamagno, Ruffo, Caruso, De Luca, Ponselle, Destinn, Ober, Schumann-Heink, Matzenauer, Lilli Lehmann, Flagstad, Pinza, and a host of others far too numerous to mention — all possessed voices of compelling power and vibrancy. Those who have been reputed to be outstanding vocalists have always had big, resonant voices of wide range and exceptional flexibility. This rule must always obtain, for resonance, the basis of all beautiful singing, is synonymous with power. Flexibility and an extensive range are a direct outgrowth of having established conditions of resonance within a balanced registration. (See Chapter VI on Vocal Registers.)

'LOUD' vs. 'BIG' TONE

In any discussion of tonal volume a very real distinction should always be made between a 'big' tone, or one that is well resonated, and a 'loud' tone, which is nothing but noise. 'Loud' singing is both inartistic and injurious to the voice and is to be avoided at all costs. A 'big' tone is the very essence of musical quality and indicates that the tone is being well resonated. As a sound phenomenon the two are direct opposites, both as to cause and effect.

The reaction of the vocal response to these two qualities of sound is interesting to observe. With the 'big' tone the scale of intensity is always smooth and even throughout the entire range of the voice. Singing of this kind is marked by a notable absence of struggle and effort, while the vocal compass is usually ample for the performance of moderately difficult music at least.

When the technique is 'noisy' all this is changed. The scale of intensity becomes decidedly unbalanced. Most of the volume is concentrated in the upper middle part of the voice range and often attains a degree of power that can only be matched by the unpleasantness of the quality. The highest tones of the voice, together with a large segment of the lower portion of the range, will be weak and entirely out of proportion to the rest of the voice. To force either weakened area without making a fundamental change in both the mental and the physical approach only leads to throatiness of the most extreme kind.

In addition to the handicap imposed by the vocal deficiencies already mentioned, the 'noisy' singer is compelled to make other sacrifices that further detract from his performance. All ability to 'color' the vowels and to create atmosphere and mood is necessarily surrendered to a boisterous and aggressive style without artistic merit. When a voice is 'noisy' all efforts at interpretation are circumscribed by the limited resources at the singer's command. Because of the excessive 'drive' and 'push' needed to support tones of this type, hoarseness due to strain frequently develops and the voice becomes rough and uneven.

RESONANCE

The reason a well-resonated tone always leads to opulence and 'bigness' is due to the very nature of resonance itself. As resonance is one of the primary goals of every known system of voice training, it will be profitable at this time to review the acoustic principles involved.

In tone production the vibration of the vocal cords produces sound waves. These waves travel by means of alternate condensations and rarefactions, i.e., a series of rapid contractions and expansions, of the surrounding air particles and pass through the cavities formed by the throat and mouth.

The position of the throat and mouth cavities set by the singer as he makes the necessary adjustments to establish the vowel forms a column of air. This column of air has a natural speed of vibration. When a sound wave is produced by the vocal cords whose frequency corresponds to the natural speed of vibration of the cavity that has been shaped, the tone is reinforced and becomes louder.

Before it becomes possible to resonate tones over a wide pitch range the conditions of natural frequency must be variable. As minute changes in the size and shape of the larynx, and especially the post-nasal pharynx and laryngeal pharynx which constitute the principle chambers of vocal resonance, may be made by the singer, these readjustments permit such changes to take place. Because he is able to do this the vocalist is capable of singing resonant tones over a wide pitch range.

The air in the cavity shaped by the chambers of resonance, in addition to being responsive to conditions of natural frequency, also vibrates in sympathy with the harmonics, or overtones, within the fundamental vibrations determining pitch. This again increases the intensity of the initial source of vibration and further amplifies the tone. Therefore, a big tone, or one indicating that a condition of resonance has been established, is one of the desirable goals of singing.

Although the early teachers could have known nothing of the acoustical rules governing resonance they certainly must have recognized the unmistakable quality of a resonant tone when they heard it. The natural tendency of all well-resonated voices to 'flow' doubtless proved a determining factor in making *legato* singing one of the constant aims of their instruction. Resonance is the 'drawing out of all the voice' spoken of by Mancini as being one of the initial steps to be taken in Bel Canto procedure. Resonance and 'big' tone are synonymous.

When a correct technique of tone production is used, the voice not only acquires power of vibrancy over a wide range of notes but is also capable of extreme agility. The performance record of all great singers of the Bel Canto era was so notable for prodigious feats of agility and for electrifying coloratura that little needs to be said in support of the view that this was one of the goals toward which their teaching was directed. Vocal flexibility, however, together with a wide vocal range can only be attained *after* certain conditions have been satisfied. These features of the well-used voice are the *result* of an efficient co-ordination of the vocal organs, and should never be considered a direct cause.

Having established the goal of power, range and flexibility as the ideal toward which Bel Canto training procedures were directed, we now must determine the *means* by which this goal was realized. It will be the purpose of this book to show that resonance, a wide vocal range and extreme flexibility may only be realized *after* certain technical conditions have been established. These conditions of technique are (1) purity of vowel quality and (2) correct registration.

CHAPTER IV

BASIC PRINCIPLES OF BEL CANTO

The first step in the vocal development of the student in accordance with the principles of Bel Canto is to learn the rudiments of music. According to Caccini and Tosi the one indispensable part of every vocalist's equipment was to learn to read music accurately at sight and to acquire a complete familiarity with interval relationships.

Simultaneously with this basic instruction all students were taught the first elements of voice production and management. The utmost care was taken to instill the ideal of tonal perfection and vowel purity, known to be so beneficial, so that this concept constantly remained uppermost in the student's mind. Tosi said, 'Let the master be careful that his pupil's tones, when singing solfeggi, are produced purely.' From the earliest lessons 'purity of intonation' was stressed and continued throughout the singer's career as the first requisite to beautiful tone.

Some estimate of the soundness of the musical instruction available to the singers of this period may be made on the basis of the following excerpt from François Raguenet's appraisal and comparison between the singers of France and those of Italy. Raguenet (1660-1722) was a scholarly French priest whose treatise on this subject was discussed by Oliver Strunk in the July 1946 issue of *The Musical Quarterly*. Referring to the exceptional musicianship of the Italian singers, Raguenet commented that 'we are not to wonder when we consider that the Italians learn music as we do to read; they have schools among them where their children are taught to sing as soon as ours learn their ABC's; they are sent thither whilst they are very young and continue for nine or ten years, so that by the time our children are able to read true and without hesitation, theirs have been taught to sing with the same judgment and facility. To sing at sight with them is no more than to read with us.'

Subjects other than sight-singing were, of course, a vital part of every vocalist's education. Instruction in the harpsichord, as well as in theory, composition and literature, was considered an indispensable part of every singer's background and occupied an important place in his instruction.

In his *Historica Musica*, published about 1624, Bontempi records an impressive description of the daily curriculum set up by his teacher Mazzochi:

'One hour in the morning was set aside for difficult passages, another for the practice of shading, another for singing before a mirror, in the presence of the master, in order to acquire a good position of the mouth and a pleasing attitude in singing. In the afternoon a short time was devoted to the study of the theory of music, then an hour was employed to put counterpoint to a *canto fermo*, and in another, again, the master explained verbally the rules of counterpoint, whilst the pupils put them into practice by writing. In a third hour reading was practiced. The rest of the day was spent in practice of the harpsichord, or in the composition of a psalm, motet, or canzonet, according to the capacity of the pupil. On the days when the pupils were allowed to go out, they used to pass through the tower gate, called *Angelus,* near the Monte Mario, where there is an echo; there they used to sing, whilst the echo returned their errors to their own hearing.'

When the intensiveness of this course of study is contemplated it will be readily acknowledged that the singers of the seventeenth century were thorough musicians, and it is little wonder that so many of them became supremely great vocalists. Unlike the majority of our singers today, these singers mastered every phase of the vocal art *before appearing in public*. Also unlike our singers of today, because they fully mastered every phase of a correct tone production their voices withstood the rigors of constant use. The vocal history of the first Golden Age of Song is replete with the names of singers who performed far into the winter of their lives without audible evidence of the quality or the freshness of their voices having been impaired.

Knowledge of fundamentals, together with the perseverance to master them, is the key to success in singing. Instrumentalists often set an excellent example for the vocalist to follow, especially with regard to their constant reviewing of the fundamentals of their technique.

A concert pianist who has long been a friend of the author sometimes tells the story of his first coming to New York to attend master classes in piano technique. With fifteen years of arduous study and preparation behind him he somewhat justifiably thought he had mastered the basic requirements of piano playing. To his surprise and dismay he was at once restricted to playing the most simple scales in the slowest possible tempo for the first three months, and only slightly more difficult passages during the following quarter. The result of this procedure, however, soon became evident in the more complete command over the resources of the instrument he gradually achieved.

This experience is a perfect example of the meaning of intelligent study and practice. Nothing is too trivial and unimportant to dismiss lightly, and this illustration shows the painstaking effort necessary to become an accomplished technician. Only through a complete control over the mechanics of tone production is it possible for the performer to reveal successfully the subtleties of phrasing and the variety of mood inherent in all great music. The artist who wishes to excel must ever review the fundamental principles underlying technique, first in order to acquire skill and facility, then in order to retain it.

Nothing is more important to the vocalist than the faithful reviewing of the fundamentals of tone production. Rote singing of scales and exercises is worse than useless, and, unless fundamentals are understood as well as practiced, absolutely nothing productive can be accomplished. Mannstein, in his *History of Song*, stressed this when he contended, 'It does not matter how *much*, but *how* we sing.' This is a very important concept of voice training. Scales and exercises are valueless in themselves. What really matters is the *manner* in which they are performed.

The training procedures devised by the early masters were intended to form correct habits of singing from the outset by combining sight-singing with tone production. Every scale and interval was required to be sung in a slow, deliberate manner, with the greatest care taken of the way each note was produced. Tosi summed up this phase of Bel Canto instruction when he stated, 'Let the scholar be obliged to pronounce the vowels distinctly. If the fault is not the master's, it is the singer's, who has not got out of the first lesson.' This is where the emphasis in singing should ever be placed, for without vowel purity it is impossible to arrive at a sound basis for producing a beautiful tone.

Research carried on in recent years by the Bell Telephone Laboratories and Electrical Research Products, Inc., as well as other companies interested in radio communication, has resulted in findings that substantiate the purely empirical observation of the early teachers of singing as to the value of vowel purity. Extensive studies of vocal tone relative to its quality have been carried out by sound engineers. In this work they have been aided by the availability of the acoustic spectrometer, and a combination of both the crystal analyzer and the level recorder for measuring intensity.

According to the acoustician the term 'quality' is used to denote the harmonic composition of a complex tone; that is, the arrangement, points of concentration and general distribution of the overtones with relation to its fundamental. Every sung tone has its distinctive quality, and this quality is determined by the number, frequency, and relative intensity of its component parts, i.e., energy distribution of the overtones within the fundamental. Each tone finds the energy distribution assembled into groups, so that certain areas of possible overtone content are strengthened or weakened at the expense of others. Each concentration of frequencies is called a 'vowel band,' and these 'vowel bands' are heard as a particular 'vowel quality.'

Partials, or overtones, present in the tone, but lying outside the vowel band itself, impart additional characteristics to the tone such as 'brilliance,' 'shrillness,' or 'thickness,' etc., according to the manner of dispersal. Any distortion of the harmonic pattern automatically detracts from the clarity of the tone produced, which in turn distorts the vowel quality. Quality, and 'vowel quality,' therefore, is entirely dependent upon the harmonic distribution as it occurs within the tone. When the acoustic conditions are right, the vowel is pure and the tone rings with real resonance. Control over the harmonic distribution may be maintained by the singer by means of vowel shading, or tone 'color,' and registration. When the laws of acoustics concerned with the composition of a complex tone are satisfied, purity of intonation follows and a pure tone is produced. Therefore, what is called a 'pure vowel quality' represents a condition of agreement between our mental concepts of quality and the laws of physics.

The constant striving of the early masters of singing toward the goal of 'vowel purity,' therefore, was in effect an effort guided by instinct whose purpose was to duplicate a favorable acoustic condition. To form a 'pure' vowel is to set the vocal organs in a favorable adjustment, and this adjustment then awakens a desirable harmonic response increasing the beauty and purity of the tone quality. This is the only means at the singer's disposal for gaining a satisfactory control over the acoustical condition of his voice.

Not only Tosi, but Caccini, Mancini, Doni, Herbst, Bovicelli and Zacconi — all important teachers of Bel Canto — laid down similar rules relating to vowel purity. The first exercises given to students were comprised of the smallest possible musical figures. Single tones were commonly used for a beginning; then, as the student succeeded in grasping the underlying principles involved, the exercise was gradually extended to include three tones, a triad, or the five-tone scale. The *accentus* was frequently used and its value further enhanced by the fact that it was also readily adaptable as a preliminary study in 'divisions,' which was an early musical custom of breaking up a slow, stately melody by adding embellishing figures. The guiding principle in all early procedure, however, remained fixed regardless of the exercise employed. Always the plan was to reduce each problem to its simplest terms, so that every detail of tone production could be given the attention its importance demanded.

FIGURE A: THE ACCENTUS

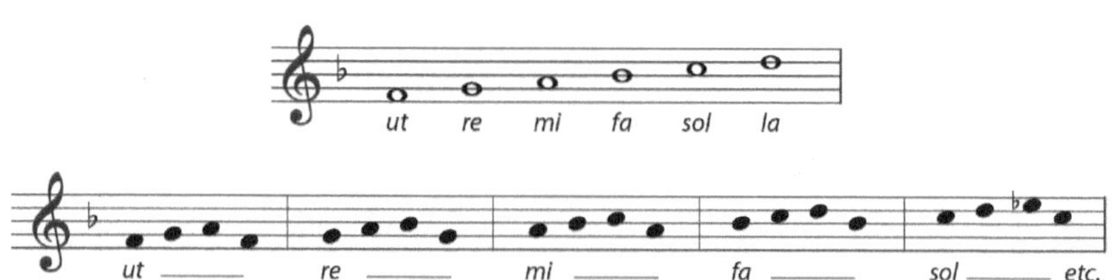

Fig. A. The accenti, as found in Johann Crüger's Preceptæ Musicæ Practicæ Figuralis, 1625.

The development of a basic vocal technique by means of slow, sustained exercises is extremely good pedagogy. The student, with time at his disposal to think the problem through, may concentrate on attacking each tone cleanly, avoiding slurring or jerking. He may fix his attention on the selection of an appropriate quality or shading of the vowel; he may give close attention to the posture of the body, mouth and head, as well as to the desired intensity, without slighting any detail that is of importance. This gives the beginner quite a lot to think about and demands all his concentration until habit patterns are formed and the muscular response to the mental picture becomes a conditioned reflex. Rapid scale passages are inappropriate as they only increase the difficulties to be overcome and help the singer to form, rather than to avoid, careless vocal habits.

As the ability of the student approached a more advanced stage of technical development subsequent exercises were planned with a view to extending the range, leading, as Tosi suggests, 'insensibly from the easy to the difficult.' Never at any time was there an inclination to hurry or to try to accomplish everything at once. Only a natural growth was encouraged and the voice was never forced beyond its immediate capacity for improvement.

After the *accentus* and exercises of similar type had been thoroughly mastered the simple turn and trill were taught. This was already an advanced stage of development and was not entered upon until register co-ordination and purity of intonation were well established. After the fundamentals of the trill and turn had been thoroughly absorbed and integrated, instruction was given in ornamentation and embellishment. Mancini advises that 'when a student has succeeded in fixing and sustaining his voice he may start on a cadenza, but it should be a short one.' Agility was recognized as a result rather than a cause of correct technique and, consequently, not to be given prominence until a very advanced stage of development had been reached.

The great *diva* Mara (1749-1833), who was an outstanding representative of Bel Canto singing, attributed her phenomenal vocal control to the religious observance and practice of this prime fundamental of singing instruction. Moore's *Encyclopoedia of Music*, published in 1854, records that 'we know from her own assurance that to confirm the true foundation of all good singing, by the purest enunciation, and the most precise intonation of the scale was the study of her life, and the part of her voicing upon which she most valued herself.' Mara, who had been well trained in the early tradition of Bel Canto, knew the test of the truly great technician and was aware that mastery of fundamentals was what counted most. An interesting anecdote highlighting this attitude toward singing is told of Mara. A friend once recommended in extravagant terms a young singer to the great *diva*, enthusing about her marvelous facility and extraordinary ability to sing the most taxing coloratura passages with ease. 'Yes,' Mara interrupted to ask, 'but can she sing six plain notes?' Mastery over absolute fundamentals is essential if the singer desires a reliable and durable voice.

CHAPTER V

THE MENTAL CONCEPT

From the foregoing it is evident that the training procedures adopted by the early Italians began with the development of a correct concept of tone quality. Fundamentally, this concept was one where a beautiful tone was regarded as being the result of a correct functioning of the vocal mechanism, while tones of ugly quality were attributed to a faulty muscular coordination, i.e., imperfect technique. A tone was considered beautiful when 'pure,' and 'purity of intonation' was known to be inseparable from 'pronouncing the vowel distinctly.'

The advice to 'pronounce the vowel distinctly' has been interpreted by many to mean that precise enunciation of consonants should be given preference over other considerations. Instead of treating the articulatory processes and the physical act of producing tone as two separate units of the whole, many teachers mistakenly believe that the natural consequence of clean articulation is firm, round tones of beautiful quality. This practice has led to an exceedingly unmusical vocal style called 'diction singing.' Singing of this kind amounts to little more than reciting the words at different pitch levels.

The evils of diction singing cannot be exaggerated and are most harmful. Everything that is basic in tone production, namely, legato singing of full, round tones of pure vowel quality, is too often sacrificed to 'mouthing' the words and overemphasizing the articulation.

When considered from the viewpoint of art and musical interpretation 'diction singing' is a hindrance. Correct tone production is always accompanied by freedom of the mouth, face and eyes. This means that the tone must be absolutely independent of any 'set' mouth position, and that the mouth is not to be used to resonate the vowel or control the tone, but only to aid in articulation. Were the tone quality dependent upon the position of the mouth as in diction singing, any movement from that position would automatically destroy the resonance adjustment while progressing from tone to tone and from vowel to vowel. This accounts for the clipped, non-legato style, so essentially unmusical, of the diction singer.

When the first steps taken by the early teachers in developing the voice were discussed in Chapter IV, it was discovered that only the most elementary musical figures, mainly solfeggi, were used so that the attention of the student could be centered undividedly on 'singing the vowel purely.' Following the inculcation of a correct concept of tone production, Tosi observed that 'the scholar now having made some remarkable progress, the instructor may acquaint him with the first embellishments of the art, which are the appoggiaturas.'

Some idea of the careful attention to detail given throughout all periods of Bel Canto training may be realized from Tosi's statement. Notice that it is only after *remarkable* progress has been made that the simple turn and leaning tones are taught. As the instruction always led 'insensibly from the easy to the difficult,' the next step was teaching the trill and easier thematic variations. Tosi then goes on to say: 'After the scholar has made himself perfect in the shake and the divisions' (and this is yet a more advanced stage than the trill), 'the master should let him read and pronounce the words.'

In this advice of Tosi's the exact reverse of the procedure adopted by the exponents of 'diction singing' is recommended. The practical course to follow in voice training is to first perfect the 'purity of intonation' on all vowels and at all pitch levels, and then later include the articulation of consonants.

To master the Bel Canto style of singing, everything must be made subordinate to a free flowing, legato vocal line with every vowel perfectly formed and executed. Nothing must ever be permitted to disturb or interfere with this. After the student has mastered the art of producing his tones purely, and as a second step learned to articulate cleanly, then the listener will be able to distinguish every word, get every subtle inflection of tone color, and find the inner meaning of the text reflected in the singer's facial expression. Without this kind of vocal freedom there is neither an art of singing nor an art of interpretation.

Tosi was even more explicit with regard to his injunction to 'pronounce the vowel distinctly' when he said: 'Let the master attend with great care to the voice of the scholar, which should always come forth neat and clear, without passing through the nose or being choked in the throat.'

This statement shows that Tosi heard a sung tone in two different ways. Clear tones, together with those that were nasal or throaty, were heard as quality characteristics. In addition, however, these quality characteristics were associated with, and credited with being due to, certain specific conditions within the vocal organs themselves. These conditions involved muscular tensions and were recognized as either interfering with or contributing to vocal freedom.

In searching for the means by which vocal freedom may be achieved the teacher of singing must choose between two possible approaches. He may attempt to obtain control over the vocal mechanism directly, or he may seek to achieve a satisfactory solution to vocal problems by indirect methods of procedure.

An example of an attempt to gain a direct control over the vocal organs is shown by the student who has been taught to arch the soft palate, raise the uvula, draw in the pillars of the fauces, adjust the tongue, fix mouth positions, or by lowering or raising the position of the larynx, and/or by methods of throat massage.

The alternative to the training given by the proponents of 'direct control' methods is that practiced by the early teachers of Bel Canto. It was their position that quality at any given time represents, and is equivalent to, a *temporary* condition of the vocal organs. Experience had shown that the quality of the tone produced could to a considerable extent be changed by altering and adjusting the 'vowel quality' and by balancing the vocal registers. As a direct result of this indirect approach new and far more beneficial arrangements within the vocal organs themselves always resulted. To sing an absolutely pure vowel carries with it the assurance that the vocal organs are in proper adjustment.

The inherent wisdom of the attitude toward voice training developed by the teachers of Bel Canto is more fully realized when we comprehend the complexity of the inner working of the vocal organs. The following description of the vocal action (actually only a part of that action, however), is reviewed by E. W. Scripture in his *The Study of Speech Curves*:

'Physiologically stated, the action for a vowel is as follows: each glottal lip consists mainly of a mass of muscles supported at the ends and along the lateral side. It bears no resemblance to a membrane or a string. The two lips come together at their front ends, but diverge to the rear. The rear ends are attached to the arytenoid cartilages. When the ends are brought together by the rotation of these cartilages, the medial surfaces touch. At this time they are stretched by the action of the cricothyroid muscles, which pull apart the points of support at the ends.

'In this way the two masses of muscles close the air passage. To produce a vowel such a relation of air pressure and glottal tension is arranged that the air from the trachea bursts the muscles apart for a moment, after which they close again; the release of the puff of air reduces the pressure in the trachea and they remain closed until the pressure is again sufficient to burst them apart. With appropriate adjustments of the laryngeal muscles and air pressure this is kept up indefinitely, and a series of puffs from the larynx is produced. The glottal lips open partly by yielding side-wise, — that is, they are compressed — and partly by being shoved upward and outward. The form of the puff, sharp or smooth, is determined by the way in which the glottal lips yield; the mode of yielding depends on the way in which the separate fibers of the muscles are contracted.

'These puffs act on the vocal cavity, that is, on a complicated system of cavities (trachea, larynx, pharynx, mouth and nose) with variable shapes, sizes and openings. The effect of the puffs on each element of the vocal cavity is double: first, to arouse in it a vibration with a period depending upon the cavity; second, to force on it a vibration of the same period as that of the set of puffs. The prevalence of one of the factors over the other depends on the form of the puff, the walls of the cavities, etc.' (48).

In making a choice between the scientific approach to voice training and the psychological method of the early teachers of Bel Canto it is important to remember that one is dealing with a muscular organization. Because the vocal organs are adjustable and inter-adjustable by a complex system of muscular contractions, it is essential to discover the extent to which these contractions are susceptible to regulation and control. When the problem is approached from this viewpoint it will be noted that two types of physical action influence tone production: one, a muscular organization subject to conscious and direct regulation; and two, a muscular organization that is involuntary, that is reflex and independent of volition.

Learning to sing would present no problem at all if the sounds produced by the vocal organs were the product of a directly controllable muscular action. If such were the case, methods could be quickly devised whereby singers could be developed who could stand on a par with the greatest instrumentalists and there would soon be a great Golden Age of Singing such as the world has never known.

Even a casual appraisal of the muscular action responsible for the production of vowel qualities as outlined by Professor Scripture, however, speedily dispels any idea of the plausibility of singing by direct control. The 'rotation of the arytenoid cartilages,' the 'appropriate adjustments of the laryngeal muscles,' the 'stretching action of the crico-thyroid muscles, which pull apart the points of support at the ends,' and the antagonistic muscular contractions causing both opening and constrictor tensions of the throat — these are all functions which lie beyond the singer's power of direct volition.

As the co-ordinate action of these muscles, together with many others, determines the efficiency of the vocal response, voice training procedures must be designed to obtain control over all involuntary acts of the muscular system involved in phonation and induce them to respond properly. As neither the student nor the teacher possesses the ability to directly control involuntary actions, this control must be gained by indirect methods of approach. Thus the problems encountered in singing are psychological. not physical.

The difference between a direct and an indirect control over the vocal mechanism may be made clear by an illustration. A teacher could possibly explain to his student that pitch in singing is established by the speed of the vibrating vocal cords. 'Now,' he may request, 'vibrate your vocal cords 256 times per second and produce middle C.'

A direction of this kind is, of course, meaningless and completely beyond the student's power of voluntary execution. By associating the speed of the vibrating vocal cords with its corresponding pitch, however, the teacher immediately finds the way open to achieve a direct result by approaching the problem indirectly. By instructing the student to sing middle C, a voluntary act he is capable of performing, the physical condition sought after as desirable has been met.

What has been lost sight of in present-day training methods is that just as the speed of the vibrating vocal cords has its equivalent expression in pitch, so every other phase of mechanical action has its corresponding quality. The segmentation of the vocal cords, together with a proper position of the pharyngeal and adjacent cavities, is responsible for producing vowel sounds, just as the distribution of the tension engendered by the contraction of the muscles stretching the vocal cords to regulate pitch results in peculiarities of sound commonly called 'registers.' To the extent that these adjustments have their equivalent expression in quality, so then they themselves may be regulated in terms of quality. Quality in this sense, of course, is used to mean 'vowel quality,' or 'pronouncing the vowel distinctly.'

The skill of the early instructors of Bel Canto, therefore, rested with their ability to associate tones of any given quality with their corresponding physical adjustment with accuracy. They knew that 'nasal' and 'throaty' qualities were due to interfering tensions and, besides being ugly, were detrimental to the voice. They also knew that the effort to produce a tone of pure vowel quality invariably set up the preliminary conditions necessary to correct the fault.

The principle that was implied rather than stated in teaching Bel Canto, therefore, was that the physical adjustment of the vocal organs is largely responsible for the quality of the tone produced. By asserting mental control over the student's concepts of quality, expressed as a 'vowel quality,' the teacher is able to correct every type of vocal fault.

Once the student has learned to gain control over different sounds representing vowel changes he has learned to directly control the involuntary muscular action of the vocal organs. When Tosi warned against singing 'through the nose,' or having the tone 'choked in the throat,' while offering the constructive suggestion that the tone pass 'free and clear' with the vowels 'produced purely,' he implied that the change in vowel quality would establish a more healthful and beneficial physical adjustment of the vocal organs themselves.

There is no question but that this latter viewpoint is the one generally supported by the early teachers of Bel Canto. They were without knowledge of acoustics, physiology and related sciences. All that could have been known was that each of the tones described by Tosi had a distinctive quality, one sounding 'nasal,' another 'throaty,' while a third was 'clear and pure.' Experience alone had evidently proven that the surest way to counteract the injurious and ugly effect of throatiness or nasality was by having the student *reverse his technique* by 'pronouncing the vowel distinctly.' To do this is to perform the physiological opposite of the 'throaty' or the 'nasal' tone quality. The first definite stride forward is made in voice training when the vowels are made 'pure' and this practice, together with registration, alone leads to the purity of intonation known to be so beneficial to the voice and the very foundation of beautiful singing.

It is impossible to overemphasize the importance of listening carefully and analytically to every sound produced in singing. Learning to sing well is in a large measure dependent upon the cultivation of aesthetic principles, and the student must become hypersensitive to perfections and imperfections of the mechanism as they are revealed and exhibited by the vowel quality.

De Bacilly, a teacher of singing who taught in Normandy during the seventeenth century, wrote a book called *Curious Remarks on the Art of Singing Well*. In this work he discusses the attributes of a talented singer. 'Hearing is a special gift,' he writes. 'There are many kinds of hearing, and these are seldom united in the same person. It is this endowment alone that leads to accurate singing. In order to become a good singer, three different gifts of Nature are requisite; viz., voice, ability, and ear or intelligence — advantages which the ignorant do not rightly discern, in that they attribute all merit to the voice alone. The most absurd question in the world is: How long does it take to learn the art? That depends entirely upon talent and ear.'

Enrico Caruso was one who believed in the importance of intelligent listening and, as he was self-taught, is an example of the progress that can be made in exceptional cases on 'talent and ear' alone. When asked, in an interview with Harriette Brower, what in his opinion constituted the first requirement for vocal success, he replied, 'Intelligence and a good ear. Listen to yourself and your ear will tell you what kind of sounds you have been making.' Intelligent and *realistic* self-analysis was the first reliance of this great tenor in matters of tone production.

This incident with Caruso is a perfect illustration of Tosi's meaning when he said, 'When a beginner has long practiced pure intonation, sustained notes, trills, phrases and well-expressed recitative, and considers that the master cannot be always beside him, then he should recognize that the best singer in the world must ever be his own pupil, and his own master.' Objective criticism, subjective analysis, and a clear mental picture of pure tone quality must ever be the sole reliance of the *mature* vocal artist. This goal should be the primary aim of all vocal study.

The question arising at this time is again related to quality. Never should the self-analysis of the performer be concerned with the commonly understood meaning of quality as vocal *timbre*. Instead, every effort should be directed toward achieving the 'purity of intonation' which can only be realized by purifying the vowel quality. A complete mental picture is one which includes tones of pure vowel quality combined with pitch, duration and intensity. In singing a musical phrase this concept must include, before the first note has been sung, the entire group of tones comprising the musical phrase, and an exact image formed as to the dynamics, scale contour and vowel qualities to be used. To dismiss, or overlook, any of these elements of good singing by directing the attention to quality as an end in itself will only serve to destroy the purpose of singing.

Learning to sing well demands of the singer a highly developed sense of timing and co-ordination among groups of muscles whose action is extremely complex. What is meant when it is said that the condition of the voice is heard through its quality is that the type of muscular co-ordination prevailing at any given moment influences and determines the quality that is produced. Depending upon the efficiency of the muscular response, the quality will either be distorted, or free and pure.

An example illustrating this viewpoint is provided by the singer who has a throaty technique. Normally the constrictor muscles of the throat should be relaxed in singing, but the 'throaty' singer inverts this procedure and creates an abnormality by bringing these muscles into tension. Whenever such abnormalities occur, the quality of the tonal emission is altered and changed into an ugly, constricted quality. No longer is the voice free and of beautiful quality and resonance. Now the tones emerge with difficulty and appear to be choked off in the throat. The result of throaty singing is a tone both painful to listen to and uncomfortable to produce.

Tosi was undoubtedly aware of the damaging effect of throatiness. When he observed that some tones issued forth 'neat and clear,' while others impressed as being 'nasal,' or 'choked in the throat,' the deduction must have been made on the basis of analyzing the tone quality and relating its quality characteristics to a probable physiological cause.

As the singer cannot voluntarily release a constrictor tension of the throat muscles as a conscious effort of will, any correction that is to be helpful must be made by demonstrating the nature of the vowel distortion caused by the throatiness. Then it must be shown how, by producing a purer vowel quality, this condition may be rectified and the constrictor tension of the throat muscles released. To make a change of vowel quality that excludes all throaty sounds, automatically sets up a change in the physiological condition of the vocal organs.

To change the conditions causing the 'throaty' tension to activate, however, it would be futile to direct the student to 'open the throat,' or to 'release the tension on the throat,' or even to 'relax the throat.' Any direction that encourages the student to think about muscular actions in the region of the throat or, indeed, anywhere else, only leads to an increase in the constrictor tensions already present, and makes the performer even more acutely aware of a phase of singing to which he should be oblivious. When muscles are forgotten and the attention concentrated on vowel quality, then the voice will immediately show an improvement. The natural tone quality will be revealed and the tone production will steadily become freer and easier.

Many volitional acts, of course, lend themselves favorably to developing the voice. The teacher is free to experiment with the position of the tongue, not to set up a supposedly ideal condition or adjustment, but to institute a change designed to break up habitual mouth formations. The posture may also be corrected, together with the position of the head and mouth. Various degrees of intensity may be used to alter the ratio of registration and create a more favorable balance between the chest and the falsetto registers. The breathing may be explained and all high chest positions avoided. As no two voices are alike technically, whatever arrangement is used depends entirely upon individual circumstances and the need of the moment. The essential purpose of any direction, however, is to change the existing coordination so that a new adjustment may be made which will be a reversal of the old.

The ability of the singer to produce sounds of widely dissimilar qualities, even with the beginner of meager technical facility, will be more thoroughly comprehended after Chapter VI (The Vocal Registers) is studied. Suffice it to say at this juncture that the falsetto, the 'feigned voice' and the chest register, each of which is a part of every voice, regardless of type, open the way for innumerable physical adjustments of a beneficial nature when properly developed. Skillful employment of these resources enables the teacher to gain an almost absolute control over the vocal mechanism and makes it possible to correct wrong adjustments and generally re-arrange the technique of tone production.

One of the essentials of good singing illustrating this principle is the necessity for raising the uvula away from the base of the tongue, as the latter widens the opening above the larynx by arching toward the soft palate for the higher tones. To make this gesture when it does not occur naturally is difficult, although it may be accomplished after months of tedious practice. The undesirability of this approach, however, is made evident by the fact that the device inevitably leads to a 'throaty,' mechanical, and stilted tone production far removed from beautiful singing.

A more practical way of achieving the same result, and to do it by natural means, is to sing the tone in either the pure falsetto, or in the 'feigned voice.' Immediately upon having done this, the tongue assumes its proper position and the uvula shrinks and disappears into the raised and arched soft palate. *This occurs automatically as a reflex action!* Thus, by learning to perform voluntary acts which awaken a favorable response of those parts of the vocal organs whose action is reflex and not subject to direct control, both the student and the teacher are able to command all the essential features of vocal technique.

Other phases of singing are analogous to this example. Vowels are sounded by the segmentation of the vocal cords, but the singer would be foolish if he were to attempt to consciously adjust their position in sounding the vowel. The vocal cords are stretched by the contraction of the cricoid and arytenoid muscles, neither of which can be directly controlled. It is the purpose of vocal study, however, to gain this control, which may only be had by combining natural intensity levels with pure vowel qualities, and by establishing a proper ratio of registration.

Once the student has learned to distinguish the subtle differences between desirable and undesirable shades of vowel quality and is able to produce tones that are 'free and clear' with some consistency, he is on a path leading to beautiful singing. Intelligent practice over an extended period of time gradually forms habit patterns and the vocal organs begin to respond correctly without conscious effort.

When a stage of training has been reached where the voice is produced spontaneously and without conscious effort, the singer is free to give his entire attention to musicianship and interpretation. Habit patterns of the kind described are known as a *conditioned reflex*, which is the only sound basis for a reliable and consistent vocal technique. Mannstein had this in mind when he said, 'It must be remembered that by practice all art becomes second nature after long continued study, so that the experienced artist thinks, not of the manner and the means of execution, but devotes himself entirely to expression without fear of singing wrongly.' Long continued study devoted to working out the principles of Bel Canto will achieve this result. What is most important to retain is the knowledge that only the *right kind of practice* counts.

Singing, then, at its inception begins with a mental picture of sound. The successful vocal technician is one who has learned to control his voice by a mental process, i.e., by thinking correctly in terms of sound. The first and most important step to be taken in voice training, therefore, should be directed toward an immediate attainment of this objective. Excepting in cases where there is a marked physical disability, the way in which the muscular system responds is almost entirely due to the clarity or opaqueness of the mental concept. All subsequent vocal control originates with the thought processes engendered at the outset of voice training.

The several phases of singing that should comprise the mental concept as it pertains to tone quality are expressed in terms of vowel, intensity, duration and pitch. Every sung tone contains these elements. As each is variable and self-contained, any one part may easily be separated from the whole and treated independently as an individual unit. The vowel may be altered, the pitch raised or lowered, the duration changed, and the intensity regulated to almost any degree, depending upon the need of the moment and the development of the mechanism itself. Registration, of course, is likewise subject to direct regulation and plays a most important role in readjusting the co-ordination of the vocal organs. When properly handled, these readjustments lead to exceptional vocal progress.

The importance of this approach to singing is that every phase of the tone quality may be regulated and performed as a voluntary act by the student. By changing the quality in this way the teacher is able to rebuild the entire physical co-ordination of the vocal organs and cause them to operate more freely, thereby helping the student to produce tones with greater ease, increased resonance and remarkable beauty.

The vocal ideal expressed by Bel Canto indicates that the early teachers of singing were keenly aware of the psychological implication of their instruction. The basic assumption upon which they founded their instruction was that the voice is clear, resonant, flexible and of wide range only when it is being properly used. From the decided emphasis placed on 'singing the vowel purely' and 'purity of intonation' it is evident that resonance, flexibility and voice extension were considered wholly dependent upon the student's success in learning to produce tones of clear quality. The other features that are a part of every well-used voice naturally followed in the wake of this procedure.

The idea that resonant, flexible tones extending over a wide pitch range is indicative of an efficient vocal response is certainly well founded. Resonance over an extensive compass demands a high degree of muscular co-ordination. The vocal registers must be in perfect balance and well developed, while the intuitive adjustments of the chambers of resonance for tone amplification must be precise and unrestricted by interfering muscular tensions. The ability to accomplish this is in direct ratio to the freedom of the vocal organs.

To accept the advice of the early teachers of Bel Canto regarding 'purity of intonation' and acknowledge the benefit to the vocal organs derived from this practice is to arrive at a new understanding of the meaning of singing. To say that a beautiful, tone is clear is to say that it is free of throatiness, shrillness, nasality, thickness, or any other forced, unnatural, imposed quality. By exercising the voice on pure vowel sounds, thereby strengthening the proper muscular co-ordination, a condition of resonance is induced and gradually established. By associating this quality of resonance with his prior concept of vowel purity the singer is ultimately able to gain an absolute control over the vocal resonators themselves.

Control over the resonators is gained first by correct thinking, and then by correct practice. As the singer learns to hear his voice more and more in terms of vowel quality, and the tones become resonant and flexible, the habit patterns that are contracted ultimately cause the vocal organs to respond automatically to the mental impetus. Through repetitive experience the singer will become increasingly sensitive to the proper 'feel' of the tone. He will learn that there is a real difference between the control that comes from obtaining a 'hold' on the tone, and the distress and struggle caused by a constriction. Singers so trained will perceive that every feeling of comfort or constraint is accompanied by its characteristic quality, either in the form of vowel purity or vowel distortion.

By controlling the vowel quality in this way the path is opened for the singer to gain a direct control over the operation of the vocal mechanism itself. Vowel purity and beauty of tone, therefore, are the equivalent of an efficient and healthy condition of the vocal organs. As the unique quality of a beautiful tone represents a factual condition transcending matters of personal taste, opinions related to voice quality must be made to conform to these conditions. The art of learning to sing is, in the final analysis, the ability to reconcile any disparity that may exist between the laws of function to which the body is subject and those aesthetic principles subscribed to by the mind.

In setting an ideal of tonal beauty as the basis of their instruction, the early Italians succeeded in developing an ideal of tone production that was both physiologically healthful and artistically satisfying. Diverse opinions may be entertained as to the probable quality of a beautiful tone, but it is an incontrovertible fact that a truly beautiful tone not only possesses a rare quality but also a faculty for overcoming vocal difficulties with consummate ease. An exact parallel is always found to exist between the quality of tone produced and the efficiency of the production itself. For this reason the really well-produced voice is not only beautiful but durable and thoroughly adaptable to artistic expression.

Every voice is capable of producing many varieties of tone quality. The selection of the quality to be exercised and developed is left to the aesthetic judgment of the teacher, and it is for him to decide which of these qualities is produced with relatively less constriction or distortion of the vowel quality. By cultivating that particular quality and at the same time offering constructive suggestions for avoiding mannerisms, the first step, and one that will show an immediate improvement in tone quality, will have been made toward the goal of vowel purity. If the teacher is sensitive to tonal imperfections and sufficiently ingenious to invent devices that will rid the voice of less desirable qualities, the technique of the student is improved and the 'natural' quality gradually revealed.

When an appropriate corrective device has been used the voice will always respond readily and show an immediate improvement in freedom, clarity and resonance. Therefore, every direction that is given must have an objective and be designed to bring about a change leading the student one step nearer the ideal technique. Improvement in singing should begin at the very outset of training, and the process of learning to sing is a consistent and regular betterment of technical facility, not a sudden blossoming that takes place after years of work.

Like all other activities requiring skill and fine co-ordination, singing demands discipline and hard work of those who would seek for mastery; and while some are fortunate to be gifted by nature with a near perfect co-ordination, others must devote considerable time to attain this goal. The only encouragement for the aspirant is the fact that, if he is well taught, every passing week, month and year will find a gradual improvement in his singing. This improvement should continue until a real Bel Canto technique has been mastered.

Acquiring a proper attitude toward voice quality is the first great obstacle to be overcome in vocal study. The most difficult thing to realize is that under no circumstances during the instruction should an attempt be made to predetermine the natural quality and *tessitura* of the voice. Quality is not something that is 'made,' or artificial. Genuine quality, or 'natural' quality, is determined by the general anatomical structure of the individual combined with peculiarities of temperament. The thickness and length of the vocal cords, the size and shape of the cavities of the throat, mouth and head — all contribute to a state of being that is. The way the instrument is used, however, determines to a very great extent the ultimate quality of the emission. According to the efficiency of the vocal response this will either be a true likeness or a poor imitation of the natural *timbre*. As the true quality of the voice is almost always an unknown quantity, because of mechanical imperfections within the instrument, no attempt should ever be made to cultivate what is thought to be the natural *timbre* of the voice. Only by purifying the vowel quality can this be revealed.

That the early masters employed a psychological approach to vocal pedagogy may be deduced from Tosi's statement on the subject of vowel purity. In this counsel is to be found a satisfactory solution to the problem of setting up an idea in the mind of the student which he may voluntarily perform, yet which also reacts favorably upon the involuntary muscular organization of the vocal organs.

The full import of Tosi's advice becomes more forceful when considered in its practical implications. As the direction concerning vowel purity is more specifically given to include the degree of loudness, posture, and exact shading of the vowel, a tangible and constructive element enters the instruction. The student has been given an idea, i.e., the creation of a pure, undistorted *vowel quality*. Fixing his attention upon this idea of quality expressed in terms of vowel, he will, instead of producing a 'made' quality artificial to his voice, create a genuine phase of tone color, unaffected and not in any way 'put on.' This is the initial and most important concept in voice training.

While in pursuit of this goal of vowel purity it is impossible to be too emphatic in cautioning the beginner against a premature attempt to extend the voice range. Extension of the vocal compass is not the purpose of preliminary training. Before the student should be concerned with reaching high tones, or singing rapid scale passages, he should first master that which is relatively easy. After he is able to produce clear tones with some consistency, then the extension of the range is to be considered. To paraphrase Mannstein, 'It does not matter how *high* the tones are that we sing, but *how* we sing the high tones.'

The advantages gained from an early development of the idea of singing with the mental processes concentrated on vowel quality are many. But it is not only because of its beneficial effect on the vocal organs alone that this concept of singing is important. Artistic singing entirely depends upon an ability on the part of the performer to create a variety of moods by means of 'tone color,' or vowel shading. Therefore, by developing a sense of vowel consciousness, serving to eliminate erroneous concepts of 'quality,' the student is also helped to become familiar with the tone colors that will later form the media of his artistic expression.

'IMITATION'

In developing new concepts of tonal values and relationships it is often helpful for the teacher to encourage the student to analyze examples of characteristic tone qualities such as 'thickness,' 'shrillness,' 'nasality,' 'throatiness,' etc., and to draw his attention to the many possible faulty combinations of registration. Examples of this kind may either be provided by another student or by the teacher himself. This practice frequently accelerates progress, especially with those of real talent, but care must be exercised in its administration.

When it is thought expedient to develop the student's imitative faculty to engender new concepts of tone qualities, the thought must constantly be uppermost in mind that the student is *not to try to imitate the teacher's voice* or manner of tone production, but only to become aware of its characteristic quality and constitution in terms of registration and vowel purity. To consider the tones produced by any singer worthy of direct imitation, however perfectly his voice may be used, is only to condemn the imitator to mediocrity. Every voice has its own individual quality, and this quality must be brought out by means of registration and vowel purity rather than be a carbon copy of a teacher's faults.

The proper use of the imitative faculty was well understood by the early teachers of Bel Canto. According to Johannes Hiller, *How To Teach Refined Singing* (1774), the mental approach to the problems of voice training is of inestimable importance. 'Example,' he found, 'does more than instruction, for it excites emulation, increases the desire to learn, and leads the beginner by a short cut to the point at which he would arrive but slowly by means of a dull lesson. The singer must become accustomed in due time to think for himself and to search out for himself. Thus the hidden treasures of the art will gradually be revealed to him.'

Mancini's work included an important reference to the use of the imitative faculty and re-emphasizes the desirability of creating mental concepts of vowel quality. 'I do not doubt,' he remarks, 'that any master whose pupil holds his mouth badly and sings faulty, or impure, tones will say at once, "that is not the correct position of the mouth which I taught you. Those tones are nasal, etc.", 'but I am certain that so slight and superficial a correction as that would not suffice to inform the student what is wrong. An easy method, from which I have always obtained good results in getting my students to understand their errors, is to imitate with my own voice the fault of the pupil. Then he recognizes his own error, be it singing through the nose, or in the throat, or with a crude or heavy tone. Hearing his faults imitated by the master he will notice them in his own singing and will confess and condemn those errors which he would otherwise never have observed, nor confessed, nor condemned to himself. And lest you believe this method of imitation was my discovery know that it was practiced in Rome by the celebrated master Fedi.' (33).

In a sense, imitation as described by Mancini amounts to nothing more than ear training which by illustration creates an awareness of the quality, character and general utility of the various types of tone that may be produced. Notice that Mancini does *not* suggest that the student follow his example. Voice training is largely a process of advancing from the known to the unknown. Eliminate the basic faults, heard as vowel distortions, and the natural quality, or *timbre*, which is invariably the unknown quantity, will reveal itself. In this way 'purity of intonation' will gradually be achieved.

After the student has begun to cultivate tones that are beneficial to his voice by avoiding 'throatiness,' 'nasality' and other common faults of production, a long stride will have been made toward establishing a solid and secure technique of tone production. Used in such a way, 'imitation' supports what has already been said about the importance of the mental concept in singing, and also supplements Tosi's dictum concerning the basis of all good vocalization: 'The master must be careful that his pupil's tones, when singing solfeggi, are produced purely. He who has no sense of hearing should not attempt either to teach or to sing.' And the same writer again: 'A young beginner in the art of singing should try, as often as possible, to hear the most celebrated singers and instrumentalists. For by observing their execution he can derive more benefit than any instruction.' Musicianship, phrasing, interpretation, and a clear mental concept of a pure, undistorted vowel quality may all be partially achieved by carefully analyzing the superior examples provided by the great artists.

In adapting the singer's faculty for imitation to the voice- building process, therefore, it must never be supposed that the student is to sound like the teacher. Nor is he to imitate another's voice quality or mannerisms in any way. Mancini explicitly stated that the *faults were to be mimicked* by the master, so that the student by listening could appraise them and learn to avoid those qualities in his own thinking and singing. Sing the vowel and sing it purely, and throatiness and nasality will find no place in tone production. Throatiness and vowel purity are antipathetic and cannot be present in the tone at the same time.

The basic principles of a sound vocal technique have now been outlined. While forming the basis of all good vocalization, these procedures are, however, somewhat limited in utility. Applied to voices that are already quite well used, these principles alone would be sufficient to maintain the voice in fine condition and even improve its performance to a considerable extent. With voices not so well used, however, these principles by themselves are not enough. What is needed with the average student is a complete vocal transformation. The voice parts must be strengthened, brought into balance and taught to co-ordinate effectively. This is only possible by carrying over these first principles of singing and applying them to the mechanism of the registers.

CHAPTER VI

THE VOCAL REGISTERS

The subject of the vocal registers has long been a favorite topic for speculation and debate, and contemporary theorists are widely disagreed as to their probable nature, number and cause. These disagreements have grown out of the ability of the human vocal organs to produce a variety of sounds of contrasting qualities.

Several factors combine to create dissimilar qualities. Principal among them are those of temperament, the size, shape and condition of the vocal organs, the combination and proportion of vocal faults, and the mechanical response of the vocal organs as they adjust to meet changing conditions of pitch, vowel and intensity.

In the present discussion only the purely mechanical aspect of tone production is of immediate interest. What must be discovered is the extent of the relationship between possible mechanical readjustments and their equivalent expression in sound. Other questions naturally follow. Is it true that all voices respond to similar mechanical laws? Do mechanical readjustments affect quality? If so, why should certain resultant qualities be called registers? Is the voice comprised of but one register, or is it made up of two, three, four, or even five? Or, as some suggest, is it incorrect to think of registers at all? As these questions strike at the very foundation of the voice-building process it is imperative that a satisfactory answer be found.

The early teachers of Bel Canto had very definite ideas concerning registration, but not until the middle of the nineteenth century was any effort made to give a logical explanation of the phenomenon. Before that time all reference to registers acknowledged prevalent characteristics of sound quality rather than specific mechanical associations. Thus, the early teachers spoke of the *voce di petto*, or voice of the chest, and the *voce di testa*, or voice of the head, without concern for the mechanical implications of their terminology. The mechanics of tone production as the expression is understood today never engaged their interest. As one of the last of the direct lineal descendants of Bel Canto, Blanche Marchesi said, 'When I was a child I well remember that such terms as vocal cords, larynx, etc., were completely unknown.' (36). Unknown, that is, to teachers and students of singing.

According to Manuel Garcia the younger, a register is a series of homogeneous sounds produced by one mechanism. These sounds differ essentially from another series of sounds equally homogeneous produced by another mechanism. Each register was held to display definite modifications of timbre and strength.

Emil Behnke, in *The Mechanism of the Human Voice*, advances the same opinion and says that 'a register is a series of tones which are produced by the same mechanism.' (3).

These two statements concerning registration reflect a gradually changing viewpoint. Whereas the early instructors had been content to familiarize themselves with the effect of the registers on the quality of the tone produced, supposedly more progressive elements became increasingly interested in purely physiological causes.

The expression 'vocal register' is derivative and was originally used by organists to describe those changes of quality caused by setting up different 'stop' combinations. When it was discovered that the voice was capable of making widely divergent sound qualities, it seemed both practical and appropriate that each group of like sounds should be referred to as a 'vocal register.' As with the organ, the vocal registers appeared to owe their peculiar and distinguishing qualities to different types of mechanical action.

An interesting parallel is to be drawn between the skilled organist and the voice teacher, for just as the organist is able to judge the approximate setup of the organ registration by listening to the sound quality of the instrument, so, too, the skillful vocal teacher should be able to analyze every detail of the vocal technique by observing the relative development and balance of the registration as expressed in the quality of the tone produced.

If there is a 'lost secret of Bel Canto' it is to be found in the knowledge of the functional interrelationship between the vocal registers which Sir Morell Mackenzie, the eminent British surgeon, declared to contain 'the whole secret of fine singing.' (32).

This statement by Mackenzie would perhaps be even more accurate if it were broadened to include *all* singing, good, bad, and indifferent, as all sounds produced always reflect the efficiency, or lack of it, of the register action.

Other factors, of course, play an important part in determining the ultimate quality of the tone produced, but such faults as 'throatiness,' 'nasality,' and 'thickness,' will always be found to operate within the register action itself. Therefore, these impurities of vowel quality must be corrected together with the development of the register action, at one and the same time. This approach to voice building gives every exercise a twofold purpose: (1) the strengthening of the individual registers while in their separated form, and (2) the simultaneous purification of the vowel quality.

Sir Morell further clarifies the relationship of the register action in singing when he adds, 'strictly speaking, there is a different register, i.e., a certain appropriate condition of the laryngeal orifice for every note, but the actual mechanical principles involved are only two.' This definition should remove many current misunderstandings concerning vocal registration and open the way to a deeper perception of the meaning of Bel Canto.

In the past century numerous theorists have observed the minor adjustments that sometimes of necessity take place within but one register and mistakenly imputed these to be separate register actions. Many of these deductions have been made on the basis of laryngoscopic examinations showing that the vibrating vocal cords assume two, three, four, or even five positions in meeting changing conditions of pitch, vowel and intensity. Thus, on the basis of visual, not audible, evidence each of these segmentations is called a 'register,' so that today one is told that there are as many as five registers, 'lower thick,' 'upper thick,' 'middle,' 'lower thin' and 'upper thin.' These divisions are also sometimes known as 'big reed,' 'small reed,' etc.

How far removed from any intelligent approach to good singing this viewpoint leads may be gathered from the very adjectives used to describe these supposed registers. The low part of a well-used voice never has a 'thick' quality, nor is the upper part 'thin.' Quite the contrary, every correctly used voice is even, clear, and smoothly produced throughout its range. Any departure from this pattern indicates a faulty technique and must be presented to the singer as such by the teacher whose duty it is to rectify the condition. Ill-advised subdivision of the voice into more than two parts has only brought confusion to a subject which must remain crystal clear if real vocal progress is to be made. Common sense alone should cause the unprejudiced to favor Mackenzie's analysis.

In order to identify the two mechanical principles found by Sir Morell to be a component part of all voices, this simple experiment will suffice. Have the student progress the great scale, the male voice to proceed from a tone in the middle portion of the voice upward, while the female singer will achieve the same result by *descending* the full scale starting from the lower middle tones. The male singer should use an intensity of only medium loudness, while the female should maintain a comfortable *forte*. Any vowel may be used, but 'ah' is most practical.

Before either singer will have completed the full scale, a point will have been reached where it becomes difficult to proceed without making a complete mechanical readjustment of the vocal organs. This is the area of the register crossing, and the singer, in order to continue without strain, is obliged to make the necessary readjustment and transfer to a new register. This phenomenon takes place in every type of voice, both male and female, the only exception being those voices whose registers work together as a single, co-ordinate unit, in which case the entire voice would appear to be comprised of but one register.

The crossing point referred to is known as the 'break,' and may always be located in the vicinity of D to F above middle C. This break divides all voices into two parts. Consequently there are two registers, or mechanisms, in all voices, one called the 'falsetto,' the other the 'chest.' Vocal progress is largely determined by the teacher's skill and understanding in developing and uniting the action of these two mechanisms.

One of the first references to this vocal fact was made as early as the fourteenth century by an Italian named Marchetto who reported that one of the vocal tricks of his time was to pass from the chest register to the falsetto after the manner of a yodel. The two registers were known at that time as the *vox integra* and the *vox ficta*.

Detailed information as to the exact position and importance of the vocal registers in voice-training methods seems to be lacking, however, until Tosi offers clarifying information. He writes, 'A master knowing that a diligent soprano, without falsetto, is constrained to sing within a narrow compass of notes, ought not only to endeavour to help him to it, but also to leave no means untried so to unite the falsetto with the natural voice, that they may not be distinguished; for if they do not unite, the voice will be of divers registers and must consequently lose its beauty. The difficulty consists in uniting them.'

This opinion represents, of course, a purely empirical observation. The conclusion, however, is based upon qualified opinion growing out of experience by trial-and-error methods covering many hundreds of years. The sum of this experience had conclusively shown that certain sounds of contrasting quality were nevertheless related, and that these sounds contributed in a large measure toward building a faultless vocal technique.

A century later Mancini corroborated Tosi's statement and shows himself to be in total agreement with the precepts and traditions of the older school. Discussing the importance of obtaining a correct register action he stresses its importance to good singing by asserting that 'the voice ordinarily divides itself into two registers, one called the "chest," the other the "head," or falsetto. Every student, whether a soprano, alto, tenor, or bass, can easily know the difference between these two registers. The great art of the singer consists in acquiring the ability to render imperceptible to the ear the passing from one register to the other.' (33).

Several points of unusual interest are revealed in these two statements. First, Tosi limits the range of the chest register to a 'narrow compass of notes.' Second, as Mancini speaks of the voice 'dividing itself' he implies that a 'break' is to be located in the approximate center of the voice range. Third, and of greatest importance, is the assertion that without exception every voice classification, 'whether soprano, alto, tenor, or bass,' contains

this division, and, finally, that at some stage of training the action of the
two registers is to be smoothly joined.

Of exceptional interest in Mancini's remarks is the deliberate inclusion
of the 'head voice' and falsetto as synonyms. No longer do vocal teachers
include the 'head voice' in the same category of sounds as the falsetto, and
this misunderstanding is one of the fundamental departures from original
Bel Canto procedure. Turning to an earlier and highly authoritative source
in the work of Caccini, additional evidence is compounded to substantiate
the validity of Tosi's and Mancini's findings.

From Caccini it may also be learned that every voice classification was
known to contain two divisions and he included *falsetti* and boys, as well as
men and women. The entire section of the male voice now commonly
divided by teachers of singing into three parts, namely, chest, middle and
head, was looked upon as belonging to the *voce di piena*, or 'full voice.'

With women's voices the deep chest tones of the lower range lying
directly below the 'break' were attributed to the action of this same register
and were actively cultivated in all types of voices from the lightest soprano
to the deepest contralto. All tones lying above the 'break' Caccini grouped
together into what he called the *voce di finte*, or voice of the 'feigned'
quality.

The full importance of the *voce di finte* is a trifle difficult to
comprehend, and its position with relation to the falsetto somewhat
confusing, until the 'art of producing the voice,' or the joining of the
registers, is fully understood. The definition given by Mackenzie in the
National Encyclopedia (1886), however, partially clarifies the issue. He
states, 'The former is termed in the Italian school the *voce di petto*, or chest
register, and the latter the *voce di testa*, or head voice. To these the Italians
add another which joins the two registers and which partakes of the

character of both; it is named the *mezzo falso*, or middle falsetto.' The *mezzo falso* is identical with the *voce di finte*, or 'feigned' voice.

Now that the *castrati* have long since gone out of fashion it is not surprising that teachers of the modern age are inclined to doubt the value of the falsetto, especially the male falsetto, to a sound technique of tone production. However, when it is recalled that from the earliest times boy sopranos and male altos were in great demand as choristers in the cathedrals and churches, it is only natural that the instructors of the *Schola Cantorum* should have thoroughly studied and experimented with the vocal resources of the boy soprano whose main reliance was the falsetto register. The next logical step was to observe its presence in *every* male voice, leading to a later appreciation of its over-all importance to effective tone production.

The choice of the expression 'falsetto' to indicate the higher of the two registers proved in many respects, however, to be misleading, because its very name encourages the belief that this register is not truly a part of the mature voice, but merely the remains of the boy's voice and quite outside the province of adult singing needs. Unless this misunderstanding is corrected the singer, unfortunately, is deprived of one of the greatest assets at his disposal. Only when found in its undeveloped state does the falsetto sound like an untrue tone, but this could also be said of any tone in either register that is the product of a retarded physical development. The female chest register, normally undeveloped, convincingly proves this contention.

It would be interesting as well as profitable at this time to seek for substantiation of these theories by inquiring into those qualities of tone production admired by qualified observers and possessed by the leading singers of the Bel Canto era.

Probably the outstanding singer of any age, Farinelli was considered by historians and critics to have brought the art of Bel Canto to its greatest perfection. While noting that this virtuoso excelled in every phase of the vocal art, Mancini specifically remarks on the 'evenness of his voice and the complete union of the registers.'

Rubini, one of the outstanding tenors of the nineteenth century, also employed a technique thoroughly based on the Bel Canto tradition. It was said of this singer that 'one of the wonders of his art is revealed in the transition from the chest to the head (falsetto) voice, and vice versa. When he reaches the limit of the chest register, E, for instance, the change in entering the head voice (falsetto) is effected so marvelously that it is impossible to seize the moment of transition.'

Yet not all great singers of this, or any, era have been able to join the register action perfectly, a fact bearing out Tosi's observation that 'the difficulty consists in uniting them.' A Parisian critic, for example, wrote of the great Alboni thus: 'no doubt the admirable voice is not without imperfection; it counts several notes which are feeble and dull, notes which serve as a transition between the chest voice, of unparalleled beauty, and the register of sounds commonly called "head" tones. It is quite evident that the virtuoso glides over this little bridge of sighs with all sorts of precautions.'

The great Italian vocal teachers having left at least a crude outline of their instruction to serve as guideposts in voice building, these fundamental principles may be applied as follows: As Mancini categorically stated, 'all voices divide themselves into two registers,' the first duty of the teacher is to recognize this condition and to take proper steps necessary to establishing them in their divided form.

Once the registers have been separated the next step is to promote, by means of appropriate exercises, those quality characteristics natural to each register. The 'robust' chest register coming from the 'breast by strength' must be built up until the normal power level of the individual voice has been reached, after which this solidity must forever be maintained. The falsetto, too, must be strengthened and brought to a comparable intensity level with the chest register. After these conditions have been satisfied, then the registers are ready to be brought together and made to work as a single, co-ordinate unit.

When the teachers of the Bel Canto era noted the tendency of the voice to 'ordinarily divide itself into two registers' they provided the first positive insight into the guiding principles of voice production.

Mancini's statement, which qualifies as it defines, in one instance clearly establishes the relative position of the registers in the vocal range as, perforce, one must hold a position directly above the other, while, on the other hand, he intimates that under certain conditions this division fails to manifest itself. The exact position of the registers is, of course, fixed by the gap, or 'break' normally separating them.

The gap between the registers, prohibiting an unrestricted passage from one section of the voice to the other, has long presented one of the major difficulties of voice training. In the handling of the register 'break' lies the answer to many vexing problems of procedure, problems whose solution is not concerned with 'breath control,' or 'voice placement,' but with a thorough knowledge of the interrelationship and interdependency of the two registers.

According to the early masters, traditional voice-training procedures largely centered around the development, purification, and gradual unification of the registers. Mancini particularly stressed the fact that both registers were invariably a part of every voice, regardless of type and classification, and made it very clear that there is no functional difference between the soprano, alto, tenor or bass voices. All properly used voices were known to obey the same mechanical principles and the only difference between the male and the female voice is that women, because their vocal organs are roughly one third smaller, sing an octave higher than men.

The perfectly used voice, therefore, should offer a definite pattern of scale contour and dynamics which should serve both as a model of attainment and a gauge of ability. To a very considerable extent this pattern of scale contour and dynamics is determined by the conformation of the blended registers.

With the division of all voices into two parts, or registers, one may readily perceive the vast differences of technique made possible by discrepancies in the balance and development of the registers alone. Few singers, whether by chance or through ignorance, ever employ a technique utilizing the fullest resources of the vocal mechanism. In almost every case these limitations have been deliberately imposed because of a failure to recognize the necessity of developing both the chest and the falsetto registers as two co-equal units comprising a whole.

The absolute lack of uniformity so prevalent in the present-day singer's performance is very largely the failure of modem voice-training methods to develop the two registers in conformity with Bel Canto procedure. As the ability to sing smoothly and evenly, and to swell and diminish with ease and freedom, as well as produce full, resonant tones, is almost wholly dependent upon a correctly developed registration, it is important that this phase of vocal training be restored to its rightful place in future instruction.

Although there are innumerable possible combinations of balance within the registration, these may be reduced to five general categories. They may be listed as follows:

1. A state of perfect co-ordination where each register has been fully developed and smoothly joined.

2. A desirable, but not ideal, condition where both registers are used with an audible gap separating them.

3. A less desirable condition where the falsetto is used alone and the chest register is excluded.

4. An equally undesirable condition where the chest register is used alone while the falsetto is excluded.

5. The last possible arrangement is the most undesirable by far and finds both registers joined together, seemingly as one, before each register has been fully developed, purified, and properly joined together.

The first category of registration is, of course, very rarely encountered, as this technical condition represents an ideal vocal production. A few singers within recent memory have succeeded, however, in realizing this ideal, and examples of near perfect co-ordination were to be found in the singing of Caruso, Ruffo, De Luca, Matzenauer and Ponselle when they were in their vocal prime. Others, of course, could be included to extend the list, and Sembrich and Melba would be important additions.

The second general voice classification is by far the most common with singers whose vocal attainments are above the average and finds both registers participating actively in tone production to a certain degree. This condition is most promising and shows the voice to be strong, healthy, and quickly adaptable for training. Students who start their course of Bel Canto training with each of the two registers clearly defined and separated by a 'break' are already beyond the preliminary stages of training, and the teacher need only purify the vowel quality, develop each register as a separate entity, and then gradually unify their action.

The third arrangement of the registration is one where the falsetto is used to the exclusion of the chest register. After the disappearance of authentic Bel Canto training procedures, knowledge of the importance of the interrelationship of the registers became lost. As a result of this loss the disposition of the 'break' became an insurmountable vocal problem. This problem is less pronounced with male voices, but in training the female voice it has become a consistent practice of contemporary teachers to dispose of the problem by eliminating the use of the chest register altogether.

Rather than solving the problem, however, the practice of discarding the chest register and forbidding its use has only multiplied the difficulties of tone production. Deprived of the use of a vital part of the vocal mechanism, any attempt to produce the low tones of the vocal range with any degree of force or intensity instantly harms the voice. The result of this misuse causes the disappearance of high tones, displaces any semblance of a vibrato with a wobble, while the tone quality becomes strained and unpleasant as the singer continually runs short of breath.

As long as the singer who uses the falsetto register alone is content to restrain any thought of ambitious undertakings and sing within the limitations prescribed by that register, however, this type of voice may be quite durable and extremely pleasant and relaxing to listen to. Many examples of this kind of vocal technique abound, and such voices are always typified by a light, sweet quality, somewhat inclined toward 'thinness,' and extremely limited in power. In addition, the range is considerably curtailed; low notes are almost inaudible and the singer is unable to swell or diminish in the middle and low voice range without forcing. Such voices show definite promise but, until *both* registers have been well developed, hardly merit serious consideration as singers.

This condition is, of course, very rare with male singers who habitually rely on the chest register exclusively. There are, however, certain rare instances where men have exceedingly high pitched voices, both in singing and speaking, and this is entirely due to an arrested development of the chest register. Such voices are very light, 'thin,' and thoroughly lacking in substance and virility. This gives rise to the impression that the voice, if the condition is sufficiently extreme, has sustained injury.

To relieve the limitations of technique so obvious in the vocal performance of those who use but one register, it becomes necessary to make a persistent effort to reinstate the action of the one normally unused. Vigorous exercise of both registers will then gradually relieve a condition having absolutely nothing to do with the position of the tongue, 'voice placing,' 'nasal resonance,' the manner of breathing, or any other superficial detail of contemporary instruction that has been permitted to develop into what amounts to a fetish by modern teachers of singing. The problem is entirely one of register development and balance, and can only be successfully dealt with on that basis.

Although it has long been a general practice for female vocalists to avoid the chest register whenever possible, many singers of popular songs have for years reversed the usual procedure and employed the chest register when singing 'hot' jazz. To a considerable extent this style of singing reveals the natural qualities of the register as it is heard in its unco-ordinated form and constitutes the fourth possible arrangement of the registration. Voices of this kind are crude, 'shouty' and masculine. Its direct counterpart is the male 'crooner' who uses an improperly co-ordinated adjustment dominated by the falsetto to achieve sickly sentimental effects.

When Mancini drew attention to the fact that the voice ordinarily divides' he made allowance for an exceedingly small classification of singers who find themselves with no perceptible 'break' between the registers. In the first grouping it was found that voices of this kind represented the ideal vocal technique. Unfortunately, however, the registers may be blended either correctly or incorrectly. It is for this latter group that exception must be made.

An incorrect blending of the register action may either be natural or acquired. Sometimes it will have been caused by a premature effort to dispose of the register 'break,' but just as frequently it will be found due to entirely natural limitations. Voices in this condition are greatly handicapped because no progress can be made toward strengthening the registers, improving the quality, and extending the range until the registers have been separated and developed independently.

Singers who have an incorrectly blended registration that has been self-induced because of a desire to smooth out the voice are almost impossible to teach. Invariably the long-continued practice necessary to bridging the gap 'sets' the technique to such an extent that the habits contracted become sufficiently deep rooted as to be almost unbreakable, and the singer becomes incapable of producing but one quality of sound. This quality, unfortunately, is always disagreeable.

One may easily know when the balance between the unified registers is correct or incorrect by the quality, type of voice movement, i.e., whether a vibrato, tremolo, or wobble, as well as by the ease and smoothness with which the performer is able to swell and diminish.

In contrast to the quality of the well-used voice the sounds produced when the registers are wrongly joined are 'white' and without character. Usually the intensity level of the scale will be markedly irregular. Conclusive evidence, however, is provided when the attempt is made to swell from *piano* to *forte*. As this increase in intensity is accomplished by transferring from one register to the other or, more precisely, by *adding* the chest register to the falsetto, unless the registers are properly joined it is impossible to make a smooth transition or to control extremes of dynamics effectively. Very often, too, the range of the voice is seriously curtailed because of a faulty juncture.

Between the extremes of registration outlined in the foregoing every conceivable variation in balance is to be found. Indeed, so infinite in number are the possible combinations that duplications are infrequent and occur only when the technique is very far advanced and the voice types and temperament are similar.

Even a casual appraisal of the style of singing exhibited by those singers whose technique is above average efficiency often demonstrates the presence of the two registers in tone production. This is especially true of women's voices, as it is permissible, if not preferable, for them to sing in a divided registration. Taste and custom forbids this practice by the male singer, who must wait until both registers have been smoothly joined before employing them in performance. With the so-called 'Irish tenor' it is the chest register that is largely dispensed with, but more frequently the falsetto is neglected while the chest register is used exclusively. The presence of the falsetto is normally detectable in the well-used male voice, however, during the singing of soft passages. A correctly sung pianissimo is always produced in the *co-ordinated* falsetto and careful listening will reveal its true origin.

A recording made by the late Enrico Caruso on an old Opera Disc of the aria, 'Je crois entendre,' from *Les Pêcheurs de Perles*, offers a perfect illustration of the interrelationship of the registers. Because of insufficient register development at the time the record was made, the great tenor found it necessary to sing the concluding phrase of this aria with its mounting pianissimo high tones by breaking off the chest register and deliberately changing into a beautifully, but not completely, developed falsetto. The whole of the concluding phrase is then completed in this register. In a later Victor pressing of this same aria the falsetto has apparently disappeared from Caruso's singing, together with the 'break.' Yet, it is quite evident from the new quality taken on by the high tones in the newer recording that this register had not been discarded, but thoroughly assimilated and made an active part of the technique.

From many quarters the argument has been advanced that the 'break' in the voice is due to unnatural causes. If this is true, then most of the great singers of history have had an unnatural way of singing! Unfortunately, the destruction of many great and potentially great voices has been caused by foolhardy attempts to eliminate the register 'break' without having the least understanding of the urgency and absolute necessity for developing and blending the register action.

From this brief summary one may conclude that modern vocal teachers have lost sight of one of the most important elements contributing to a sound vocal technique. Whether taught as a basic theory of Bel Canto, or observed as a vital part of every well-used voice, there can be no doubt that all voices are made up of two qualities of sound, called registers, and that these two registers occupy a very important place in the voice-building process. Evasion of the problems posed by the presence of the 'break' by not using one of the registers has only led to innumerable makeshift arrangements of highly questionable expediency.

Although the teachers of Bel Canto placed the greatest emphasis on the importance of the registers it would be a serious mistake to assume that the presence of the two registers in their separated form automatically assures a correct method of tone production. Many voices that are poorly used also contain a divided registration. Any advantage that might otherwise have been gained by an initial separation, however, may be thoroughly obviated by the presence of 'throatiness,' 'nasality,' 'thickness,' or an improperly balanced registration.

Of equal importance to the setting up of a divided register action, therefore, is the assurance that within each register the vowels are kept absolutely pure, so that careless vocal habits, which are always found in the guise of vowel distortion, may be avoided, thus allowing the natural traits of each register to be revealed. Tosi's admonition that 'the master must be careful that his pupils' tones, when singing solfeggi, are produced purely' is one to be taken seriously if the student is to make real progress.

Both Tosi and Mancini were explicit in describing the typical characteristics of each register as well as the means to be employed in developing them. Tosi speaks of the extreme 'volubility' of the falsetto, as opposed to the *voce di petto*, which he described as the 'full voice which comes from the breast by strength.'

The very first step in voice training, therefore, should be devoted to finding the two registers and then exercising each in such a manner as to bring out their special characteristics. The *voce di petto*, or voice of the chest, should be encouraged to become strong, resonant and vigorously produced with the intent, as Mancini said, to 'draw out all of the voice.'

Every characteristic of the chest register finds its direct counterpart in the falsetto, which Tosi declared to possess the utmost mobility, both as to intensity and flexibility.

Because the male falsetto seldom exceeds a compass of ten semi-tones and consequently lacks room for rapid or extensive movement, the flexible quality of this register will be discovered to be somewhat less impressive in the male voice than it is in the female voice. This is especially true during the early stages of advancement, and not until the falsetto has been worked into a partially unified action with the chest register will its inherent properties of elasticity become pronounced.

The flexibility of the falsetto is shown to best advantage by the soprano voice, especially the coloratura, whose naturally high *tessitura* includes relatively few tones in the chest register, and who sings almost exclusively in the falsetto. This is so, because by far the greater portion of the coloratura vocal line lies above the register 'break.'

In the absence of a co-ordinate register action with the chest voice, the average soprano voice inclines toward lightness, flexibility and sweetness, while lacking solidity and evenly distributed power. This is true, of course, only if the falsetto is kept pure. Until such time as the chest register has been brought to a comparable stage of development, the soprano voice will remain weak and thin in the lower octave of the falsetto; low tones will frequently be inaudible and, although the singer is sometimes able to control *piano* effects, this virtue is largely offset by an inability to sing *forte* by way of contrast. The special ability of the coloratura soprano to perform exciting vocal gymnastics, however, provides a perfect illustration of the inherent flexibility of the falsetto register.

As long as the falsetto is preserved in its pure form with a minimum of co-ordinate action with the chest register, it will present, in addition to being flexible, the widest possible extremes of intensity. Starting in the lowest portion of the pure register (D, E, or F), the tone is at best soft, breathy and incapable of swelling.

Ascending the scale, the intensity of the pure falsetto register mounts with increasing rapidity until by the time the top line of the treble staff has been reached a full *forte* has already been attained, after which the volume continues to increase until the very highest tones have been reached.

On all upper tones of the falsetto the singer is usually able to swell and diminish with fluency, but once the lower middle and lower tones have been reached this is no longer possible and the singer must be content to conform to the natural contour of the register outline until such time as the proper conditions have been established for increasing its volume. Once the chest register has been properly joined this vocal limitation is overcome.

Should the attempt be made to exceed the natural limitations of the pure falsetto by forcing the lower portion of the range without bringing in the requisite amount of chest register to balance the registration, serious strain to the vocal mechanism would ensue. This disturbance of the register balance destroys the purity of the falsetto, which slowly disintegrates. Middle tones become increasingly unsteady and begin to 'wobble,' while all the highest tones become more difficult to produce, until they are finally eliminated from the vocal range altogether. All tones of the voice steadily lose in fullness and freedom.

No attempt should ever be made in early stages of voice training to 'polish' the voice, or to try to make the student meet the interpretive standard of concert hall performance. Because of the 'break' that must for some time remain quite pronounced in women's voices, the smooth scale necessary to artistic singing remains beyond the capacity of the performer. This, of course, makes singing somewhat cumbersome and awkward for some time, but once the gap has been reasonably narrowed a much wider versatility is afforded the singer and range, 'color' contrast, and a greater and more honest expression of personality may then be brought to every interpretive effort.

Preliminary studies, rather than being concerned with finished interpretive effects which the singer is incapable of executing properly, should always be devoted to bringing out the natural qualities of each register. The robustness of the chest, and the unbalanced intensity of the falsetto, should both be deliberately cultivated while at the same time the vowel quality is purified within each register.

The problem of the registers is less apparent in actual performance in the male voice than it is with the female vocalist. Forbidden by custom and propriety to use the unco-ordinated falsetto in public, the male vocalist is confronted with other problems. Chief among these is that he must be content to wait until both registers are perfectly united before having access to really high tones or pianissimo effects. Because a considerable portion of the male vocal range lies comfortably below the register 'break,' however, the male vocalist is able to sing with moderate effectiveness long before the registers have been co-ordinated. Tenors, because of their high *tessitura* extending well beyond the area of the 'break,' find this problem much more acute than do basses or baritones.

In training the voice, therefore, the intent of all preliminary exercises must be to bring the voice to a condition which might best be described as 'natural' and 'healthy' rather than 'trained' and 'cultivated.' After the registers have been properly developed the singing of high tones, loudly or softly, will become a relatively simple matter. Once the student has progressed to this point, nuance and interpretive finesse then become issues of paramount importance.

The beneficial effect of a careful cultivation of the two registers is shown in many ways and makes possible a complete transformation of the vocal technique. Mancini knew this to be so and was moved to remark that 'experience has taught us that with proper study a weak voice will be made round and strong.'

Usually either or both of the registers will be found undeveloped at the outset of training. The primary objective of preliminary training must therefore be directed toward strengthening them by vigorous exercise. Because the male falsetto and the female chest register are as a rule infrequently used, if at all, in either speaking or singing, the neglected register will always be found in a weakened condition. The advice of Mancini in such instances was to 'keep that portion of the voice which is by itself robust and sprightly and to render that other portion strong which is by nature weak.'

The first stage of training is a long one and no undue haste must ever be shown if satisfactory results are to be obtained. The second stage of training does not begin until both registers have been clearly established and all imperfections removed that might detract in any way from the purity of the vowel quality. As Tosi said, 'oblige the pupil to pronounce the vowel distinctly, or he has not got out of the first lesson!' How many singers appearing before the public today may justly consider themselves, on the basis of Tosi's statement, to have progressed beyond the first lesson?

It must be remembered throughout all stages of early register development that the student is not made to sacrifice this development in order that the voice may sound smoothly cultivated. A far better condition is one where the uneven outline of the divided registration is followed so that the voice gives evidence of being fresh and of promising vocal material. This is, of course, more applicable to women's voices than it is with men's voices.

REGISTERS AND RANGE

First to be affected by restoring the chest and the falsetto registers to their rightful place in the technique is the range of the voice. By using two registers instead of one, both male and female voices will add a group of notes embracing anywhere from ten to twelve semi-tones. With the soprano and contralto this means an immediate downward extension of the lower voice range where the chest register is operative.

As the female chest register becomes well integrated into the technique this area of the voice grows in strength, beauty and power. The falsetto, because the voice is functioning naturally, also benefits. An immediate effect of this arrangement is that the entire voice increases in range, freedom and power.

Even at the outset of training, the two registers when used together embrace two octaves or more in range. Additional training will show a steady and consistent growth until a maximum of three octaves has been reached. Because neither register is being forced or overtaxed the entire range of the voice is produced with a sense of ease and security that makes performing and listening a real pleasure.

What has been said of the female voice applies in every respect to the male voice except that the falsetto, habitually unused, must be found and made a vital and co-operative part of the voice. As is the case with the female chest register the introduction of the male falsetto immediately adds a group of tones, potentially usable, extending over some ten or twelve semi-tones.

The tones comprising the falsetto register, while unsuitable for performance until thoroughly developed, nevertheless exercise a profound influence for good upon the chest register throughout all periods of training. After the falsetto has been properly developed and utilized the chest register will, without forcing, increase in freedom, flexibility and resonance.

Like the female voice, both the upward and downward extension of the registers almost immediately includes a range of two or more octaves. With final co-ordination many more tones are added. Failure, therefore, to use both the chest and falsetto registers is inevitably attended by a loss of efficiency. The voice will suffer a decline in freedom and power. An octave of potentially usable notes is abandoned, never to be replaced by other means. Greater effort must be put forth to sustain the register that has been retained, and the severe burden placed upon it may be heard in the off-pitch and unsteady singing so frequently heard in our concert halls today.

REGISTERS AND INTENSITY CONTROL

In addition to directly influencing the range of the voice the registers also provide the only satisfactory means of controlling changes of intensity. Under ideal conditions both the male and the female falsetto play an ever more prominent part in the production of tone. This phenomenon becomes increasingly obvious as the registers begin to develop.

The effective area of operation for the chest register is circumscribed by the register 'break.' This terminating point is indicated by the permanent unwillingness of the chest voice to mount higher without being forced to do so. Present-day teaching methods seek to overcome this obstacle by 'covering' the upper tones of the chest register, by proceeding softly, or by developing 'nasal resonance.' None of these devices has proved satisfactory.

Unlike the chest register, the falsetto, as it increases in power and fullness, begins to extend its position in two directions. This occurs naturally and without resistance. Depending upon the weight of the voice, the upper portion of the falsetto rises comfortably to the vicinity of high C, while the lower extreme more and more spreads down into the chest register. Thus, there is an overlapping point from B below to E above middle C, where each tone may be sung in either of the two registers. A successful juncture of the registers may be made when a point of development has been reached where the quality and intensity of each register has been made to match at the point of crossing, or the 'break.'

Once the 'break' has been obscured, the singer is able to pass freely from one register to the other, 'imperceptibly,' as Mancini observed. It is this ability to utilize the fullest resources of both registers that gives the singer an absolute control over changes of intensity.

Throughout all periods of development the registers constantly, if gradually, undergo a change. Those qualities distinguishing the falsetto increasingly become a part of the chest register, so that to its basic 'chesty' quality is added a sweetness and flexibility together with a gain in control over changes of intensity. Concurrent with these changes taking place in the *voce di petto*, the falsetto also acquires in its turn a fullness and solidity no longer making this register sound false. It is through this interchange of quality characteristics that final co-ordination of the registers becomes possible as, obviously, both registers must ultimately sound exactly alike if they are to be made to meet on terms of perfect equality. In order to meet properly, the two registers must match in quality and intensity at their point of juncture.

With the continued development of the falsetto prior to coordination this register considerably overlaps and spreads down into the chest register. As a result of this overlapping, four or five of the upper tones of the chest register may be produced in either one of the two registers. As the upper part of the chest register is robust, while the lower part of the falsetto is soft and fragile, the blending of these two extremes makes possible a desirable versatility of tone production. The constant practice of the *messa di voce*, or swelled tone, by the early Italians was only a persistent attempt to join the action of the two registers.

After the quality and intensity of each of the registers has been made uniform, and the gap separating them bridged by the development of the 'feigned voice' (see end of chapter), the singer is able to pass freely from one to the other without fear of detection. Thus, to swell from *pianissimo* to *forte* the properly trained singer starts in the co-ordinated falsetto and gradually increases its volume until the limit of its resources has been reached. At this point the chest register is brought into action and the robust quality inherent in this group of tones then continues to increase the volume until the maximum resonance of the voice has been reached.

Passing from one register to the other by means of controlling the intensity, however, only applies to those tones lying below the register 'break.' No attempt must ever be made to pull the chest register up higher than E on the bottom line of the treble staff. Any effort to do so will only lead to forcing. All tones lying above E properly belong to the falsetto register, or the 'feigned voice,' regardless of whether they are sung loudly or softly.

Figure B shows the region of active participation assumed by the chest register and the falsetto. In this way the dominant part played by the falsetto in *all* voice types is clearly shown.

FIGURE B

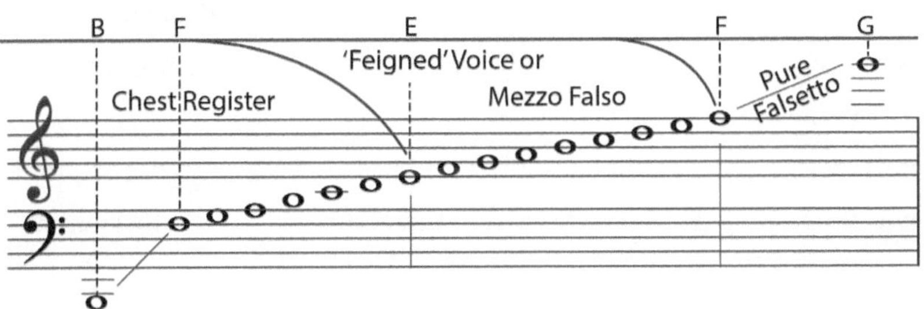

With every voice, male and female, fitting within the framework of the two-register theory advocated by the teachers of Bel Canto, the problem of working out the voice becomes greatly simplified. By establishing a clean-cut division between the chest and falsetto registers, it becomes literally possible for the teacher to take the voice apart, when necessary, and reconstruct it in conformity with a predetermined pattern known to represent the ideal vocal technique. Thus, the instrumentality is provided whereby great and technically proficient voices of beautiful quality, resonance, wide range and flexibility can be built. The only limiting factors legitimately standing in the way of the attainment of this goal are those where the pupil is deficient in talent, or, for want of skill, patience and understanding on the part of the teacher.

The early masters were, therefore, exceedingly cognizant of the vocal organs as an instrument and no allowance was made in their training procedures for quality divisions such as are accepted by the profession today. It is a mistake to be 'trained as a tenor' or 'trained as a contralto,' as there is no functional difference in voice types. All voice types are bound by the same mechanical laws, so that the basic fundamentals of tone production remain unchanged regardless of the type of voice being trained. A more constructive approach endeavors to teach the student to 'sing' rather than 'sing like a baritone.'

The only safe and practical way of determining the natural quality and *tessitura* of the voice is by a proper method of register development and by purifying the vowel quality. Then the voice will seek its own natural *tessitura* and the quality *will reveal itself*.

This process is similar to one where the surface of a forgotten masterpiece of painting has been allowed to gather dust and grime in an attic for many years. After proper restoration and the removal of all blemishes, the original will once again stand as a revelation of the creator's genius. In training the voice we must follow a similar process. In a majority of cases the natural quality of the student's voice is unknown, whereas the distortions and imperfections of vowel purity and registration are very evident. By stabilizing the registers and purifying the vowel, the natural *timbre* of the voice will reveal itself. Thus, it is usually incorrect to say that a performer has a 'poor voice,' when in reality he is simply a 'poor singer.'

Blanche Marchesi showed her thorough understanding of this phase of Bel Canto training when she said, 'Before voices can be classified they must be brought out, and by the right method, so that their quality and category may be determined. Not every voice shows at the very beginning to which category it belongs, and in such cases the teacher must proceed cautiously and not stubbornly to a preconceived judgment, from a wish to appear infallible. Unless the development is closely followed a fatal mistake is easily made.' (36).

Once the true significance of the interrelationship and interdependency of the two registers had become lost, voice-training procedures suffered a complete revision. Only one of the two mechanisms was allowed to be used or developed and, oddly enough, the same register was not retained by all voices. The falsetto was found more congenial to female voices so, consequently, male vocalists were no longer taught to use this register. On the other hand, the chest register was neglected by the female singer while the male voice uses it almost exclusively.

After it had become common practice to confine singing techniques to but one register, that which had been retained came to be divided into three sections, viz., chest, medium and head. As this division was determined by the range of the surviving register, all significance formerly attached to registration disappeared. Gradually the earlier understanding of the registers was superseded by the belief that in reality the retained register, i.e., the male chest register and the female falsetto, contained three tonal groups later described as 'low,' 'medium' and 'head.'

FIGURE C

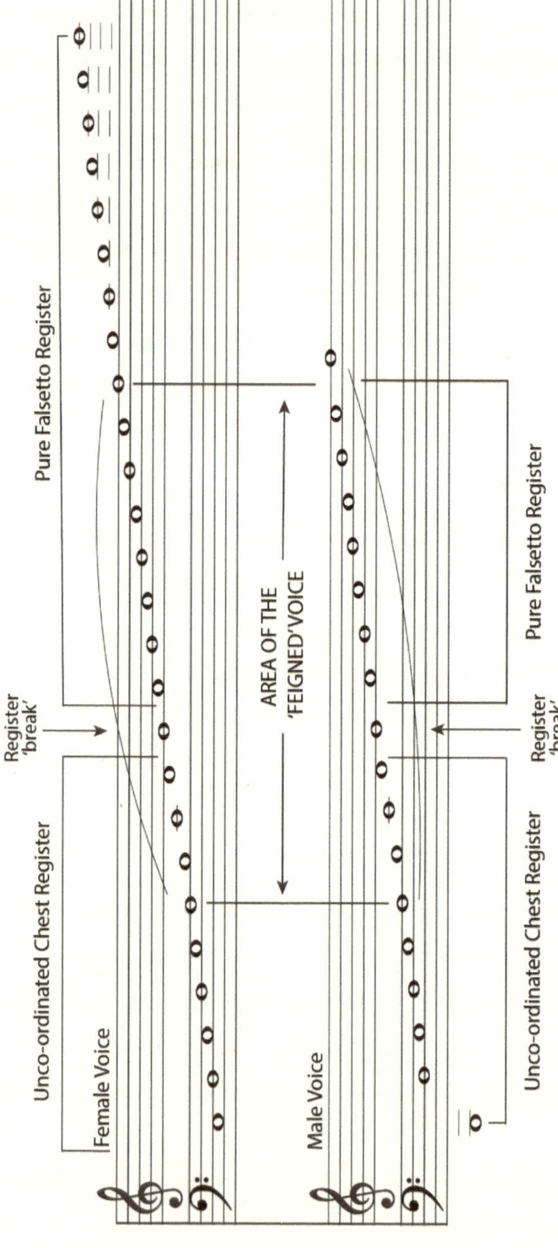

Fig. C. Showing the extreme vocal range, from bass to coloratura soprano. Here the position of the two registers, the chest voice and the falsetto, is clearly shown, as well as the 'feigned' voice, which is the only effective agency for co-ordinating the register action.

FIGURE D

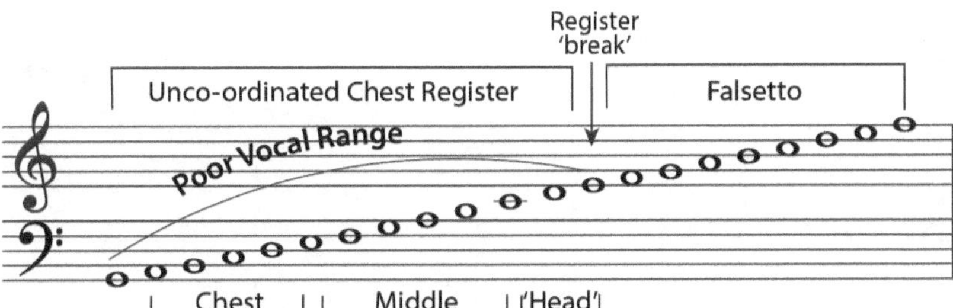

Fig. D. Vocal range of a poorly used baritone voice, illustrating the difference between present-day concepts of registration (shown in lower brackets) as opposed to 17th & 18th century practices.

FIGURE E

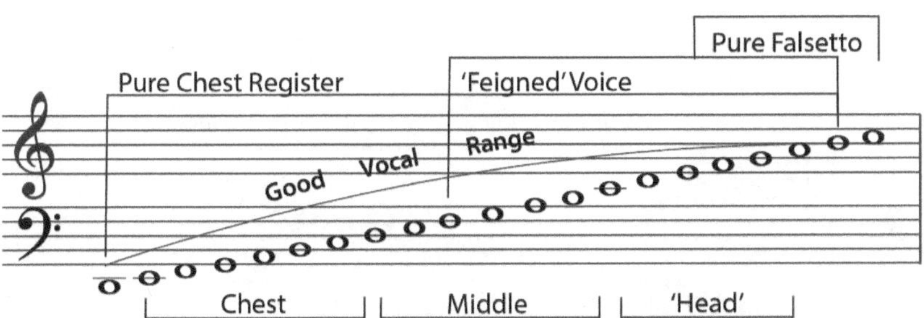

Fig. E. Vocal range of well-used baritone voice, illustrating the similarity of the well-developed 'head' voice to the area where the falsetto is dominant.

FIGURE F

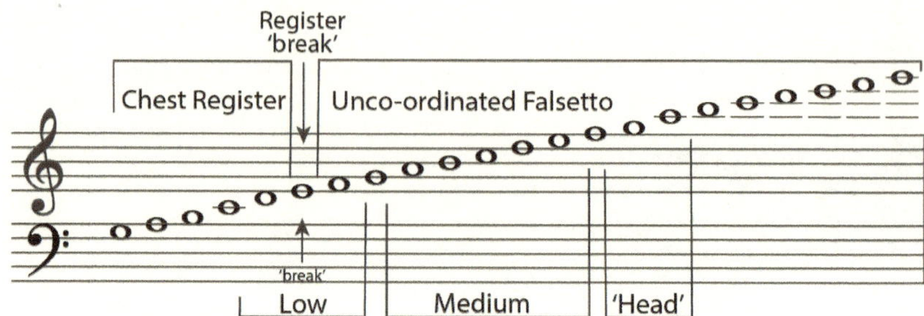

Fig. F. Soprano voice of poor range, showing the purely arbitrary division of the voice into registers (lower brackets) as opposed to the earlier understanding of registration as practiced in the era of Bel Canto.

FIGURE G

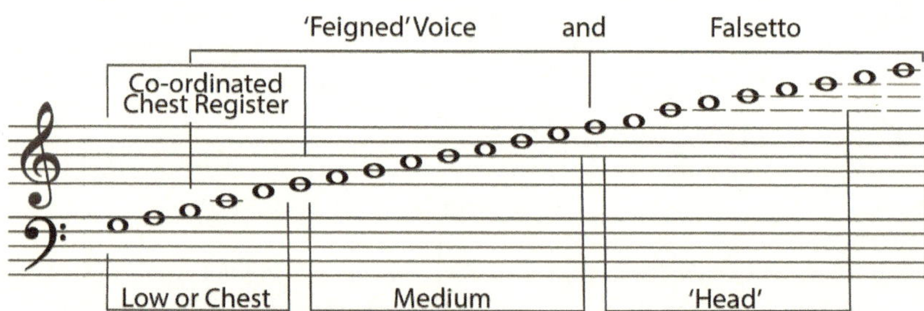

Fig. G. Showing the parallel position of the registers, low, medium and 'head,' to those of earlier usage. This is how the registers would appear in the properly used soprano voice.

The new register division, of course, is quite meaningless, as it refers to pitch ranges and not separate mechanical actions. In this context the 'head' register is not used synonymously with the falsetto, but usually indicates a 'covered placement' for the upper tones. Figures C, D, E, F and G demonstrate present-day concepts of registration as opposed to those taught by the early Italians.

In preparing these diagrams it has been thought advisable to illustrate the position of the registers in two ways. First, as in Figure C, each register is shown as it exists in separated form, i.e., as found in elementary stages of training where there is a minimum of co-ordination. Here, also, the area of the 'feigned voice' is shown, demonstrating the overlapping action which should ultimately obliterate every trace of the register 'break.' In this way both the preliminary and final stages of correct register development are clearly shown.

Second, as in Figures D, E, F and G, modern concepts of registration are contrasted with those opinions held by the early teachers of Bel Canto. These diagrams specifically pertain to the baritone and soprano voice, but the principle involved is equally valid for the tenor and contralto. Notice how closely the vocal range of the technically well-advanced singer conforms to the register outline as described by Tosi, Mancini and other early masters. Contemporary concepts of registration, on the contrary, are often highly self-contradictory and meaningless.

It is easy to see from these diagrams that the points of disagreement between the old and the present-day arrangement of the registers are far greater than those of agreement. As treated by the teachers of Bel Canto the approximate position of the two vocal registers remained constant in all voices, irrespective of whether the technique was good or bad, or the voice high or low. It is also important to observe the parallel position of the 'head' register of the male singer, who uses his voice well, with the area of tones produced by the falsetto. Thus the real difference between a poor singer and one who sings beautifully is indicated by the comparative development of the registers. A fine singer does not necessarily have an exceptional voice, but only uses his voice exceptionally well. Proper development of the registers establishes these exceptional conditions. When a corrected registration has been established the talented beginner with a poorly used voice will have been taught to sing. Basically, this is the Bel Canto voice-building process and the most intensive work over a sustained period is required for the fulfillment of its aims.

Observation based upon every-day experience with the singing voice attests to the accuracy of the register theory here advanced, especially with regard to the 'break' in all unco-ordinated voices in the vicinity of E, bottom line of the treble staff. Figure C convincingly demonstrates that the essential difference in voice types, i.e., soprano, alto, tenor or bass, is brought about by the position of the 'break' in relation to the natural *tessitura* of the voice.

As the falsetto provides the lyricism essential to every well-used voice, whenever this register dominates the technique, or the greater portion of the natural *tessitura* is included in the area of its effectiveness, the voice is said to be 'lyric.' The same principle holds true when the chest register is either overdeveloped in comparison with the falsetto, or when the preponderance of the vocal range comes within its control, except that the voice is thought to be more adaptable for dramatic effects. Because they have a greater proportion of falsetto lying within the body of their vocal range (see Figure F), the higher voices, i.e., the tenor, soprano, and especially the coloratura soprano, are inclined toward greater lyricism than the lower voices.

Qualities such as 'dramatic' and 'lyric' are, however, primarily those of temperament and the well-trained singer is never obliged to be restricted to one interpretive style. Actually the correctly used voice, because both registers have been given their rightful prominence, will include the characteristics of each as a part of the technique. Thus, the essential difference between two such great lyric sopranos as Melba and Sembrich was one of temperament, as both voices had a similar *tessitura*, were full, resonant, clear, even in scale, able to swell and diminish fluently, and possessed exceptional range and freedom of execution.

Briefly stated, the vocal pattern to be sought after should include full-bodied low tones which gradually increase in power as the scale is ascended while, in addition, the performer should possess an absolute control over changes of dynamics. When the technique fails to meet these requirements it is faulty, as either the registers lack development and are out of balance or the vowels are impure.

The effect of the registers on the various voice types will differ according to the disposition of the voice to find a *tessitura* moving away from, or toward, the register 'break'. It is with the inner voices, i.e., tenors and contraltos, that the more serious problems arise in register development. This situation is brought about because the tenor and contralto voice range straddles the register 'break', while the voices of basses and sopranos lie considerably outside. Where to some extent the soprano, bass and baritone can get along by using only one register, albeit with limited effectiveness, the contralto and tenor must employ *both* registers, or fail abjectly in acquiring the requisite skill for overcoming even moderate difficulties.

When the falsetto has been left uncultivated in the tenor voice all ease and security will disappear at F, above middle C. Without the falsetto taking an active part in tone production the tenor is forced to drive the chest register up, and by so doing destroys the free, round quality natural to that register. All that is gained by having done this is a series of 'reedy' tones extending to A flat at most, beyond which point the voice is utterly unable to proceed. There is constantly said to be a scarcity of tenor voices, but if one pauses to reflect on the great number of 'A flat' tenors, or tenors that pose as high baritones, the truth is forcefully carried home that this voice type is not so much a rarity as it is the victim of bad teaching practices.

The contralto, unless the technique is well advanced because of natural endowment, is similarly handicapped by inadequate teaching. As the voice range of the contralto, like that of the tenor, extends well beyond either side of the register 'break,' neither register can be dispensed with unless a large segment of the range is deliberately sacrificed. It has been in this manner that many potentially beautiful contralto voices have been reduced to the status of being so-called 'mezzo-sopranos,' usually an indeterminate voice of mediocre quality which is incapable of singing either the high tones of the soprano or the low tones of the contralto, solely because of improper register development.

In contrast to the tenor and the contralto voice types, basses, baritones and sopranos are sometimes able to sing somewhat effectively, even though the two registers may not be participating in tone production. The difficulty in singing above E flat so universally experienced by basses and baritones, however, is directly attributable to the unfortunate neglect of the falsetto register. The inactivity of the falsetto also deprives the voice of those characteristics of 'volubility' which Tosi and Mancini found a part of the essential nature of the *voce di testa*. As a result of this neglect, low voices are usually inclined to be inflexible. High tones attempted without proper co-ordination of the falsetto are insuperably difficult and must be forced, while all *pianissimo* effects in the upper range are virtually eliminated.

In contrast to the lower male voices the qualities of the falsetto register may be more easily detected in the soprano voice. Without using any chest register at all it is possible for the soprano to sing in the falsetto register alone from D above middle C to the D above high C, provided, of course, that the register definition is scrupulously preserved.

Using the falsetto without the help of the chest register would, obviously, seem satisfactory in view of the fact that such a wide pitch range may be covered. Unfortunately, however, singing in the pure falsetto without effective co-ordination with the chest register creates an unbalanced gradation of intensity. Because of the absence of the chest register the lower octave of the falsetto is much too weak to be effective, and the entire voice lacks 'body' and solidity. Any effort made to build and strengthen this area of insecurity without bringing in the chest register always forces the voice and is most harmful.

With the problems involved in working out the voice centering on the registers the importance of this phase of training is inestimable. Every aspect of good singing, namely, resonance, flexibility over a wide range and control over dynamics, is in a large measure dependent upon the full development and close co-ordination of the chest and the falsetto registers. The reason that students of singing are no longer able to acquire even the rudiments of a Bel Canto technique is because they are not being taught the basic principles of register management.

A successful solution to the problem of register development is entirely dependent upon an appreciation of its importance, and realization of the fact that the natural mechanical function of all voice types is identical. Both male and female voices, if they are being properly produced, will do exactly the same thing at the same absolute pitches. The only difference in function is that the higher *tessitura* of the lighter voices will include fewer chest register tones than those of lower *tessitura*. Otherwise the typical characteristics of each register, regardless of the proportionate amount used, must be successfully brought out. There is no such thing as a separate method of singing for high or low voices, but simply one correct way of producing tone whereby the natural response of the vocal organs is given free play.

When applying the principles of Bel Canto to voice training, it is important to remember that allowance must be made for the condition of each individual voice. Although the underlying principles governing the operation of the vocal organs never change, the means employed to set up a correct vocal technique may often be contradictory in the extreme. Mancini made this very clear when he said, 'the rules cannot be made general, nor can they be made to universally apply to every individual.'

In this statement Mancini is not talking about fundamental 'principles' of tone production, but 'method of procedure.' This point he evidently felt to be such an important one that he later clarified it by stating, 'It must be remarked that the quality and constitution of different voices vary, as also the degree of the faults; so it remains, beyond doubt, that although a method is a good one in itself it cannot be applied in every case with good results. This fact established, it consequently follows that each fault in the voice requires a different remedy to be applied to the origin of the fault.'

The essential truths embodied within the vagueness and obscurity of the expression *Bel Canto* will only be revealed when it is realized that this style of singing was not a 'method' or system of instruction, as the term is now understood. Actually it was a term applied to the *result* of the application of certain basic principles of tone production.

It is impossible, therefore, to acquire a Bel Canto technique by following any prescribed 'method' because all voices, while subject to identical laws of function, differ widely as to their faults. Infinite varieties of incorrect vocal production are the rule, rather than the exception, and if the teacher is to be successful these must be treated individually. In many instances it will be found that diametrically opposed directions will, when applied under proper conditions, supply the solution to a difficult problem. Against this type of instruction all 'methodic' procedures are impotent. Consequently, it may be said that there should be as many 'methods' as there are pupils.

MUTATION OF REGISTERS

The art of joining the registers so that the two work together as a single entity is the most difficult phase of Bel Canto procedure. Mancini noted that the successful juncture of the registers demanded the greatest patience. He remarked, 'It may be the case that the blending of the two registers has not yet reached an ideal of evenness, nevertheless, I beg the teacher and student not to lose faith, because I am sure in the end success will crown the effort — the other tones in the voice will be greatly benefited by this exercise.'

More specific advice as to the exact procedure to be pursued in joining the register action is offered by Giacomo Gotifredo Ferrari in a pamphlet, *A Concise Treatise on Italian Singing* (1818). He suggests that 'If he, (the student) feels difficulty in uniting the chest voice and the head voice, he must, by art, strengthen the extremity of that which happens to be weakest.' As the early Italians always considered the 'art' of singing to mean an absolute control over dynamics and an ability to swell and diminish, the inference is plain that the registers are to be joined by swelling from *piano* to *forte*.

The joining of the registers, therefore, begins by building up 'the extremity of that which happens to be weakest' which, almost without exception, will be the lower portion of the falsetto. The device invented to secure the unification of the *voce di testa* with the *voce di petto* was the *messa di voce*, or swelled tone.

The proper swelling of any tone in the vicinity of the register break is achieved by commencing the tone in the co-ordinated falsetto and then to increase its volume until the quality and intensity of the two parts that are being joined are exactly alike at their point of juncture. The 'break' itself is reduced and gradually eliminated entirely, therefore, by increasing the strength of the co-ordinated falsetto. Even after the transition of registers has been made the falsetto *remains active* while the chest register action is *added*.

In advanced stages of training the performance of the *messa di voce* must be practiced continually until there is an exact matching of both quality and intensity at the point of transition. After this technique has been mastered the 'break' disappears, and the singer is able to pass freely from one register to the other, from soft to loud and from loud to soft, without difficulty. This is the kind of technique that the early masters described as 'the art of producing the voice.' This is the singing style known as Bel Canto.

A successful performance of the *messa di voce* provides a graphic illustration of the close alliance that must exist between technically correct singing and artistic singing. Once the voice becomes free and flexible throughout its range, interpretive effects may be made because of musical necessity and not out of consideration for deficiencies of technique.

In practicing the *messa di voce* it is important to recognize five basic principles:

1. The falsetto is the dominant factor in all tones in the region of the register 'break,' and must be built up to achieve equal prominence with the chest register. The gap separating the registers should never be lessened by forcing the volume of the chest register, but always by increasing the strength of the falsetto.

2. The chest register should never be extended beyond the point of the register 'break,' but that the growth of the falsetto must be increased and brought *down* into the chest register.

3. The *messa di voce* is suitable for only two or three semi-tones comprising the immediate area of the 'break.' No attempt must ever be made to force the action of the chest register higher than its comfortable range will permit. F above middle C, therefore, is the highest note permitted

for this exercise. Above that point *all tones*, even those that ring out as a brilliant *fortissimo*, belong to the falsetto and the 'feigned' voice.

4. After the registers have been co-ordinated the falsetto does not go out of action, but continues to participate actively in tone production. When the procedure is reversed and the scale is ascended in the full voice the chest register remains active even after the falsetto has been added, but its degree of participation should never be permitted to exceed that which it achieves at the point of the 'break.' Thus, in proceeding full voice beyond the area of the 'break' the chest register 'holds,' while the activity of the falsetto and the 'feigned' voice rapidly increases.

5. The registers must match in quality and development before unification can take place.

Many variations of the basic principles of the *messa di voce* were used by the early Italians to provide variety and avoid monotony. After the comparatively easy *messa di voce* had been mastered another, and more demanding, device was employed. This was the *esclamazio viva*.

The *esclamazio viva* begins with the tone sung *forte*. Next the performer was required to reduce the volume slowly and deliberately to an absolute *pianissimo* then, in the same breath, to again increase the volume and return to a full *forte*.

As the technical proficiency of the singer advanced another and yet more difficult exercise was introduced. This was called the *esclamazio languida*. In the *esclamazio languida* the singer was required to swell the tone from *pianissimo*, as in the *messa di voce*, with a gradual diminuendo back to the soft voice added, following which the tone was once again swelled to its maximum *forte*.

Like all Bel Canto training procedures, these exercises were performed with deliberate slowness until a complete technical mastery and assurance had been gained. Mancini proffers a valuable hint as to the correct

performance of these exercises and suggests that 'the most certain means is
to hold back the tones of the chest register and to sing the transition notes
in the head register, increasing the power little by little.'

The following musical symbols will demonstrate the various exercises
growing out of the *messa di voce*:

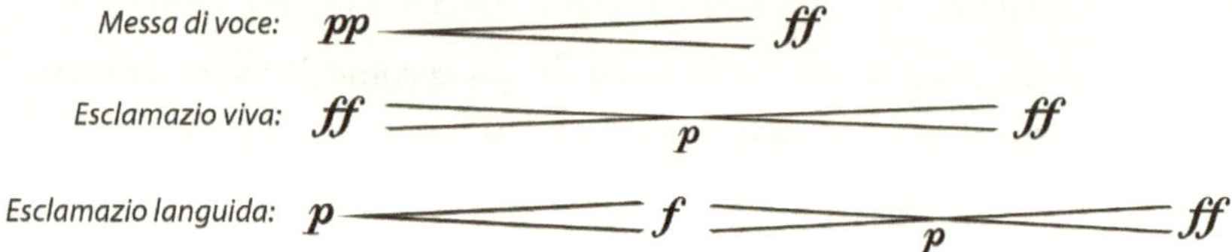

One of the most important rules to be followed in joining the
registration was first discovered by John Miksch, a teacher of Dresden who
had learned the Italian style of singing from Caselli, a pupil of Bernacchi. 'I
maintain,' he declared, 'that the joining of the registers can only be attained
through the repose of the mouth, tongue and throat whilst singing. The
slightest movement of either of these three organs disturbs the
imperceptible joining of the registers. The tongue presents the greatest
difficulty.'

The action of the tongue in singing is perhaps unique in that it
performs, or must be taught to perform correctly, two distinct functions.
The first of these is the articulation of consonants such as *t, d, I,* and *n,*
where the forward part and tip of the tongue is active, while guttural
consonants such as *k,* and the hard *g,* are made by the back of the tongue.

A second primary function of the tongue is that it must also shape at its
base to form the vowel position for the sustained tone. As these functions
take place simultaneously with the register action a series of problems arise
which must be carefully worked out if the voice is to be made responsive to
the demands of language and music.

To combat the difficulties encountered in joining the register action and at the same time make it work co-operatively with the tongue, it is best to proceed cautiously step by step. Therefore, the first task is to effect an approximate juncture on a single vowel: 'ah' is usually preferable. Later the other vowels may be included.

After all vowels have been developed to the extent that the register break is entirely eliminated, it becomes necessary to connect the several vowels together. This is done most effectively by using the five basic vowel sounds on a single tone in the vicinity of the break and by changing from one vowel to another without disturbing the legato vocal line, as 'ah,' 'ay,' 'ee,' and 'oo.' Throughout these exercises a normal mouth position must be used.

Having mastered the co-ordination of the register action on all primary vowels, the next step is to create a harmonious relationship between these adjustments and the articulatory processes, so that neither one interferes with the work of the other. This is the supreme difficulty to be overcome *after the registers have been brought to their fullest development* and made ready for coordination. This is a long range program and requires infinite patience as well as concentration of the highest order.

Once this process is thoroughly understood the oft-related and sometimes ridiculed story of how Porpora kept his pupil Cafferelli for six years on a few simple exercises scratched on a piece of note paper and then told him to 'go forth and sing, you are now the greatest singer in the world,' does not seem so ridiculous. The solution to the fundamental problems of registration *can* be worked out, and *have been worked out*, with the use of only one or two musical figures, namely, the single tone, the *accentus*, and by vocalizing the great scale, using *sol-fa* syllables. What matters, really, is *the manner in which they are sung*. And, of course, it is a matter of history that Cafferelli *did* become the world's greatest singer after making his debut.

In listing other general rules for guidance in joining the registers, it is important to be sure that the initial attack is perfect. This means that the vowel, pitch and volume must be established instantaneously. A tentative approach is fatal. Having established a clear, well-resonated tone in the co-ordinated falsetto as a beginning, the teacher must make sure that no alteration is made in the vowel quality as the loudness increases, especially as the crossing of the registers is being made. This means, of course, that the entire mechanical adjustment of the resonance cavities must remain constant throughout the entire procedure. If this is not done the exercise will fail to achieve its purpose.

In discussing the separation of the registers it was stated that the practice of increasing the volume of the lower tones of the falsetto register always led to forcing, while, on the other hand, this procedure was later advocated as the best possible way of bringing the registers together. This contradiction is more apparent than real, however, and the essential difference between swelling and forcing the registers will now be shown to depend upon the cultivation of the 'feigned' voice, or *mezzo falso* as it has sometimes been called.

THE 'FEIGNED' VOICE

Generally speaking, the nomenclature used by the early masters to describe the various effects the voice is capable of producing met with almost universal acceptance. The voce di piena, or full voice, and the voce di petto, or voice of the chest, obviously designated the same register of sounds and it is almost impossible to confuse their meaning. From time to time, however, a third group of tones was referred to as a register and was known as the voce di finte, or 'feigned' voice. All available evidence indicates that the 'feigned' voice appeared and was cultivated after the falsetto had reached an advanced stage of development.

A full comprehension of the importance of the 'feigned' voice is somewhat difficult at the present time as this vocal device has long since fallen into disuse. In reality the 'feigned' voice is nothing more than an outgrowth of the falsetto, and is an adjustment of this register giving it a somewhat 'edgy' quality of tone.

Other names have been used to describe the *voce di finte* and one that was more prominently used was the *voce di gola*, or voice of the throat. The French sometimes referred to this quality as the *voix mixte*, or mixed voice.

The remarkable and distinctive qualities of the 'feigned' voice are caused by the fact that these tones appear to contain the basic elements of both the *voce di testa* and the *voce di petto*. By combining the lyric quality of the falsetto with the 'bite' of the chest voice, the resultant combination is one that enables the singer to pass with the utmost freedom from one extreme of both range and intensity to the other.

An interesting development growing out of the use of the 'feigned' voice is that it ultimately tends to supplant, with its continued growth, all uncertainty and insecurity heretofore experienced in the area of the register 'break.' Thus, the 'feigned' voice becomes the only means by which the register action may be satisfactorily joined together, so that the singer becomes able at all times to maintain an absolute control over tone color and intensity variations at all pitch levels. The 'feigned' voice also eliminates the danger of forcing the lower range of the falsetto register.

The position of the 'feigned' voice between the registers *di petto* and *di testa* subsequently gave rise to the suggestion from numerous quarters that these tones comprised a third register, sometimes called the 'middle.' This determination proved unfortunate. First, because the expression 'middle' is too loosely applied as, strictly speaking, the 'feigned' voice does not represent the middle area of all voice types; and second, because of the

ever-present danger that its proper relationship as an evolutionary process
growing out of the falsetto is likely to be overlooked. To classify the
'feigned' voice as a separate register was not entirely illogical, however, as
this group of tones does for some time possess a distinctive quality creating
the impression that it is perhaps due to a separate mechanical action of the
vocal organs and, therefore, well within the accepted definition of a
register.

The precise position of the 'feigned' voice in Bel Canto teaching
procedures has been superbly explained by Isaac Nathan, an eminent
teacher of singing and scholar who in 1836 published a treatise called
Musurgia Vocalis. In this work Nathan provides detailed accounts of the art
of Bel Canto as it was understood and practiced in his lifetime. Of the
available references to the 'feigned' voice his is the only definitive
explanation of its position in voice culture. His explanation is as follows:

'There is a break, more or less, in the voices of both sexes, but more
particularly in that of the male, between the *voce di petto* and falsetto; that
precise part of the vocal organ where the *voce di petto* forms the juncture
with the falsetto is by the Italians called "Il Ponticello" — "the little
bridge"; and singers who can with safety carry the *voce di petto* over this
little bridge may truly sing its praises. It should be an object with the singer
to contrive to blend the two qualities of tone, at their juncture, in such a
manner, that the transition from one to the other may not be perceptible to
the ear. This cannot be accomplished without the aid of the "feigned" voice,
which may justly be considered the only medium, or vehicle, by which the
falsetto can be carried into the *voce di petto*.

'Should my observation on the "feigned" voice appear obscure, and the
tyro find any difficulty effecting its practice, or in distinguishing it from the
falsetto, which is not improbable from the seeming affinity the two sounds
bear to each other; he may at once satisfy every doubt upon that point by
exercising his falsetto on different vowels, in which attempt he will

discover it to be physically impossible to articulate the Italian broad a, but the "feigned" voice will against all resistance instinctively become the vehicle of its intonation — at this crisis the two qualities of tone must be instantly detected.

'The tyro having thus far satisfied his ear in distinguishing the "feigned" voice from the falsetto, should endeavour to blend those two qualities of tone by commencing with his falsetto upon any given sound, and whilst in the act of prolonging that sound, change the vowel without taking breath, as:

this will decidedly effect the desired union, which having been accomplished, the next object must be that of uniting the "feigned" voice with the *voce di petto*.

'Let every note be begun in the "feigned" voice as softly as possible, by swelling gently, and immediately returning to the first *piano*; as the voice increases in power and quality let the swell be increased, yet with caution; the slightest irregularity or roughness being a sign that the singer has exceeded the development of which his organ is capable.

'The greatest care must be paid to these remarks, in the cultivation of the highest tones of the voice; for as the natural compass of the *voce di petto* of either denomination seldom extends beyond ten or twelve notes, all others are properly artificial, and must be assimilated to the original by the above method — any attempt to supersede which, by forcing the chest tones, will certainly be attended by the ruin of the singer, notes that are so acquired being harsh, and incapable of colouring, and liable to disappear altogether.

'The rule experience pronounces infallible is this: — when the singer after having cultivated the lower tones, which form the basis and give character to his voice, arrives at the "break," or meeting of the registers *di petto* and *di testa*, let him proceed to the "feigned" voice alone; let him increase its power by swelling, and let him gradually unite it with the chest voice rather by its own enlarged volume than by any exertion of the latter — thus effected, the juncture will be imperceptible.* It is only by voices so formed that the higher effects of the heart can be produced — or qualities so often lauded be realized.' (42).

The foregoing account is so detailed and complete that little remains to be said either with regard to the authenticity of its being the proper Bel Canto procedure, or the urgency of a universal acceptance. It will perhaps be well to re-emphasize the advice Nathan offers concerning the chest register and his warning against forcing the upward extension of its range. This is a common practice in contemporary teaching and partially accounts for the failure of modem methods to achieve the results formerly obtained when the principles of Bel Canto were more thoroughly understood.

Tosi was also most explicit in warning against the dangers inherent in forcing the upward extension of the chest register. He pointed out that 'through want of experience, many masters compel their pupils to sustain long tones with the forced chest voice. The result is that day by day the throat becomes more and more inflamed, and if the pupil's health does not suffer the voice is ruined.'

Giusto Ferdinando Tenducci offers the same counsel in his *Instructions of Mr. Tenducci, to His Scholars*. Fourth in a list of twenty rules is this hint: 'never force the voice in order to extend its compass in the *voce di petto* upward; but rather to cultivate the *voce di testa* in what is called falsetto, in order to join it well and imperceptibly to the *voce di petto* for fear of

---

* Notice the exact similarity of this practice with the performance of the *messa di voce*.

incurring the disagreeable habit of singing in the throat, or through the nose, unpardonable faults in a singer.' (54).

Further confirmation of the beliefs expressed by these qualified authorities may be found in the work of Richard Mackenzie Bacon who lends support to their claims. Although his book is not a scientific treatise in the accepted sense of the word, nevertheless it affords considerable insight into the quality of the singer's art and the techniques employed to create that art as practiced in his own time.

Addressing himself to the problem of joining the action of the vocal registers Bacon advises, 'In this case an endeavour should be made to sing the note (meaning the transitional note in the area of the "break") with greater power in the falsetto, or less in the natural voice, in order to use both with equal facility and assimilate the tone; also continual sustaining and increasing and diminishing of three or four successive notes up and down, taking the faulty one in the middle, are the best modes of abating or obliterating the defect. All voices, male or female, should pursue this same regimen.' (1).

Understanding the interrelationship of the chest and falsetto registers, the need for their separate development and the subsequent process of unification which follows, forms the entire basis upon which all real vocal progress rests. Every other phase of vocal technique is subordinate to, and dependent upon, this. The registers form the cornerstone upholding the entire structure of the voice-building process. The extraordinary power, range and flexibility for which the voices of the Bel Canto singers were so justly famous has been a direct outgrowth of a fully developed and delicately balanced registration.

If, as the writer believes, it is desirable and essential to return again to those principles so clearly expressed in the writings of the leading exponents of Bel Canto, then it becomes necessary to prepare a complete revision of the modern pedagogical approach. The function of the registers alone, as understood and practiced by the early teachers, demands this fundamental realignment.

CHAPTER VII

SCALES AND EXERCISES

The immediate objective sought in working out any theory of tone production necessarily demands the use of scales and exercises. It is of great importance to the success of the voice-building process, however, that the value of a particular exercise is not overestimated.

Although some exercises often lend themselves better than others toward the accomplishment of specific goals it must be remembered that all are intrinsically valueless. Any exercise may be performed correctly or incorrectly and, according to the intelligence of the effort expended, can either be tremendously beneficial or entirely useless. The single tone is, of course, indispensable to the performance of the *messa di voce*, but apart from this exception one attractive musical figure will do as well as another, provided it is of simple construction and directed toward working out the problems of registration.

The careful and unhurried means employed by those who followed the old tradition has had many champions and the substance of their opinion has been given clear expression by Salvatore Marchesi. In his book, *A Vademecum for Singing Teachers and Pupils*, the noted teacher advises: 'To obtain uninterruptedly successful results teachers must present to their pupils only one difficulty at a time, and insist upon making them overcome the obstacles they encounter, by placing the same before them in a natural and progressive order. This is an immutable general precept of teaching.' (37).

Were this law, so clearly stated by Marchesi, to be conscientiously obeyed by present-day teachers of voice it would mean that an end would have to be made to the haste with which students are introduced to repertoire, especially a repertoire they are incapable of singing even adequately. While ambition is a praiseworthy attribute the cause of art would be better served if students were made to confine their ambition to overcoming those difficulties within reach of their abilities, rather than attempt arias intended for mature artists.

'In order to obtain this fundamental result of building the instrument before playing upon it,' Marchesi goes on to say, 'teachers, after employing elementary exercises to place the voice and determine the limits of the registers, must pass to the second part of the physico-mechanical work, making the pupils sing a series of plain and easy vocalises adapted to the character and compass of each particular voice, and always upon "ah." ' These are sound principles.

Continuing his outline of the voice-building process Salvatore Marchesi not only shows his thorough understanding of the principles of vocal technique involved, but rephrases ideas which are an extenuation of the principles of Bel Canto as described by Tosi, Mancini, and other early authorities. This is clearly and convincingly shown by the following:

'By singing through a series of adequate vocalises (Etudes), pupils continue to practice and perfect the transmutation and the blending of the registers. Watching and directing the voice at first under the guidance of the teacher, the pupil will by and by do this automatically, in consequence of the habit the muscles of the vocal organ will have acquired by following the mental impulses. Being strictly prepared in this way, pupils, beginning to sing with words, will no longer be preoccupied with forming or directing every single sound, or with the change of registers, but will be able to concentrate all their attention upon the clear production of the different vowels and the marked and distinct articulation of every consonant, without interfering with or disturbing the continuity of the sound.'

With regard to 'diction singing' Marchesi is also in complete agreement with the earlier teachers of Bel Canto and believed that the free emission of pure vowel sounds should always be given precedence over articulatory processes. The secondary status of articulation is explained in this way:

'The root of the tongue being firmly fastened to the tongue bone an attempt at singing with words before the action of the tongue and that of the larynx and the glottis have become independent of each other, makes the articulation of the lingual consonants interfere with the free emission of sound. Hence the absolute necessity of continuing to sing on "ah" until this independence has been acquired. If this elementary technical principle is not rigorously observed the singer will be doomed, throughout his whole career, to sacrifice the *word* to the *sound*, or the *sound* to the *word*.'

The abandonment of Bel Canto procedures in recent decades has introduced many problems of vocal technique that would never have arisen if the advice of those who truly understood the old tradition had been consistently sought out and followed. How unfortunate it is that so many really fine artists are now constrained to sing within limitations that obscure, rather than reveal, their innermost sensitivity and awareness of the composer's musical intent. Real artistic expression is only possible when the *word* is independent of the *sound*, and the *sound* independent of the *word*.

Up to and including the present time it has been almost a religious duty for students of singing to plod through progressive studies by Concone,

Bordogni, or Liitgen, as though these contained an inherent value providing a cure-all for every vocal fault. Of course, they possess no such ability. What really matters is not so much *what* is sung, as the *manner in which it is being performed*!

A common type of exercise that should absolutely be ruled out of consideration at all times is the variety devoted to the study of velocity. Hasty, robot-like, and thoughtless running through exercises and scales makes a mockery of all vocal study. Students trained in this way, unless they are already technically well advanced, can never hope to acquire a substantial or dependable vocal technique.

Singing at all times, but especially in the early stages of training when habits are being formed, requires the utmost concentration and attention to detail. Every tonal imperfection must be understood for what it is, and really basic principles of tone production applied to remedy the fault. Glossing over faults never corrects them but only serves to make them permanent.

The cultivation of habits of self-analysis and a most severe self-criticism in matters of tone production must be carefully engendered at the very outset of vocal training. The teacher should create an ideal toward which the student must strive, as well as show him the means by which these goals may be attained. Tosi summed this up beautifully when he said, 'When a beginner has long practiced pure intonation, sustained notes, trills, phrases, and well-expressed recitative, and considers that the master cannot always be with him, then he should recognize that the best singer in the world must ever be his own pupil, and his own master.'

Notice the order of progression outlined for the course of study; 'pure intonation,' 'sustained notes,' 'trills,' 'phrases' and finally leading up to 'well-expressed recitative.' Velocity exercises are not even mentioned! The safest procedure is always to sing slow, legato exercises so that the attention may be concentrated undividedly on every detail of tone production. In this way it is almost impossible to form careless vocal habits.

Other teachers of a later period who strove to keep alive the old tradition of Bel Canto singing also followed this precept. Blanche Marchesi noted that 'to obtain a clear transition from one note to the other, slow practice for a considerable time is necessary. Quick exercises can only result in blurring, not in settling, the pure intonation of semi-tones.' (36).

A much earlier writer was even more emphatic with regard to the inadvisability of cultivating agility before the technique was sufficiently advanced and 'set.' Francesco Lamperti, who was much closer to the early tradition than Marchesi, strongly urged that rapid exercises be used sparingly. 'I should recommend,' he writes, 'caution and moderation in the study of agility, as the voice by too rapid exercise is apt to become tremulous and weak, and thus, what otherwise would have been one of the most beautiful embellishments of singing, becomes one of its most serious faults.

'In conclusion, I may add that I consider the enormous quantity of exercises which one finds in many books on singing superfluous, and more likely to injure than preserve the voice, or cultivate a clear and beautiful agility.' (29).

The singing of rapid scales and exercises, even for the coloratura soprano, should be deferred until a stage of training has been reached where correct habits of tone production have made the vocal response to become almost a conditioned reflex. Even then, the student is much better off performing the works of Bach, Handel, Bellini, Donizetti, and others whose works may not only be performed in public, but also provide perfect lesson material for the advanced student. It is important to remember at all times that flexibility is a *result* of a correct tone production and *not a cause*.

Too great care cannot be expended by the teacher in guarding against his students falling into errors of concept or execution during the time devoted to the mastery of the fundamentals of singing. In this respect the advice of Sabilla Novello is very much to the point. In *Voice and Vocal Art*, published in 1856, she counsels, 'It is a great mistake for the student to commence practice unassisted; bad habits are thus contracted which the attentive guidance of an able teacher would at once correct.' Unsupervised efforts to develop technique are bound to fail of their purpose.

A more complete understanding of the work entailed in mastering the art of singing, and the care that must be lavished on every tone if the correct fundamentals of production are to be mastered, is revealed by Lilli Lehmann in her book, *How to Sing*. 'Practice,' she says, 'and especially practice of the great, slow scale, is the only cure for injuries — I often take fifty minutes to go through the great scale only once, for I let no tone pass that is lacking in any degree in pitch, power, and duration.' (30). This, from her own report, was the study of Madame Lehmann's life. How important it is to master every detail of technique! This is the reason Madame Lehmann remained throughout her lifetime one of the supremely great vocal artists of history.

Thus, the old saying that 'practice makes perfect' only holds true so long as the practice is constructive. As Mannstein said, 'It does not matter how much, but *how* we sing.' And this means constant supervision by the teacher, who must be responsible for the management or mismanagement of his pupil's vocal life.

Singing musical scales and exercises by rote has never made, nor will it ever make, a singer. The teacher who will improve the voices entrusted to his care must have a carefully trained ear, and this ability to detect, analyze and correct tonal impurities is the result of protracted study, intelligent observation and experience. For the young student to take a few lessons, receive a book of exercises, and then proceed to practice without supervision an hour or so daily what he *thought* he had learned in his last lesson is most presumptuous. Usually several years of study is required before the student is qualified to help himself.

The most effective argument against unsupervised practice, of course, is that real vocal progress demands a continual betterment of the technical condition of the vocal organs. This fact implies change. What is applicable to one stage of training does not apply to another. For example, to have a student tenor attempt to sing like a Caruso is wrong, even though the great tenor's technique is the ultimate goal of the student's instruction. Because the technical condition of his vocal organs is poorly coordinated the young student is utterly incapable of doing those things which came naturally and easily to Caruso.

Those faults of technique which handicap all beginners must be removed little by little. Therefore, vocal progress is brought about by *gradually changing the technical condition of the vocal organs.* Unless the teacher and the pupil both keep abreast with these changes progress is retarded. Thus, change is the essence of vocal progress. Unsupervised practice only prevents these changes from occurring and serves to 'set' the technique. Once the technique has been 'set' the habit patterns that have been formed become almost impossible to readjust, either mentally or physically, and the student so conditioned by hours of wrong practice is almost impossible to teach.

The first step marking the beginning of the development of a Bel Canto vocal technique has been described by Caccini who said, 'I maintain that the first and most important foundation is, how to start the voice in each register. Not only that the intonation be faultless, neither too high nor too low, but that thereby the quality of the tone be preserved.'

As the male falsetto and the female chest register are almost always weak, the best plan is to begin by strengthening the undeveloped register first. The exercise employing a single tone is most suitable for this purpose and the very first principles of tone production applied. The posture must be easy and natural, the vowel must be pronounced as purely as possible, while the intent of the proceedings should be to 'draw out all of the voice,' i.e., the exercise must be performed at a comfortable *forte*.

The precise starting point for commencing the development of the registers is indicated by the area of the 'break.' To guard against the danger of an impure registration the safest policy is to by-pass the area of the 'break' itself and begin comfortably within the limits of whichever register has been selected for development. With the male voice F or G, above middle C, is an appropriate note, while B, below middle C, is most suitable for the female voice. No effort should ever be made in early stages of training to bridge the gap separating the registers, nor to effect an interchange of quality characteristics. Each register should be clearly defined and seemingly bear little affinity to the other.

In choosing a vowel for exercising the voice, allowance must be made for the register being used, as well as certain acoustic peculiarities affecting range. The Italian broad 'a' was most commonly used, especially with women's voices. Recent discoveries by acousticians have confirmed the wisdom of this practice. Their experiments have shown that women's voices, because the area of frequency, or vowel band, determining the 'ee' and 'oo' vowels is strongly concentrated around G above the treble staff, are physically incapable of producing any clearly defined vowel other than 'a' in the upper range of their voices. Thus, as the female voice rises beyond G and A flat the fundamental, or basic, speed of vibration determining the position of the pitch in the musical scale, has passed beyond the area of frequency whose activity must be engaged to sound an 'ee' or an 'oo.'

Because men sing an octave lower than women the problem of the 'ee' vowel does not exist for them. As a matter of fact, tenors are usually inclined to favor this vowel for high tones and, because the tones in this area are in the heart of the 'ee' vowel band, they are much easier to sing than 'a.' If the technique is good it is always possible for the male voice to sing higher on the 'ee' vowel than on any other. While exercising the male falsetto, therefore, either the 'ee' or the 'oo' vowel will be found more congenial than the 'a.'

To sing a pure 'a' is one of the most difficult vocal accomplishments. Almost every early teacher of Bel Canto advocated its use whenever practicable and Lablache, the great basso, strongly urged his students to 'sing a great deal on "a," because it lays bare defects, and is for that reason the most efficacious means for overcoming them.'

After a start has been made toward separating the registers, the problem more and more centers around the means to be employed in developing them. Tosi urged the teacher to 'render that portion strong which by nature is weak,' while Mancini said much the same thing when he instructed the teacher to 'draw out all of the voice.'

Francesco Lamperti, however, left much more detailed directions governing different stages of development. He first emphasized that all tone should at the beginning be emitted with the full voice, never by commencing softly and attempting to swell. This latter practice, he declared, would hinder progress and the loudness should always be made to remain constant until the technique was well advanced.

While pointing out the advantages to be gained by developing the voice by means of vigorous exercise, Lamperti nevertheless cautioned those who would teach against forcing the voice. Progress must never be hurried. After the pupil has become proficient, then the first elements of tonal nuance are introduced by reducing the volume of the tone started full voice and gradually diminishing to *piano*.

Like many other authorities on the subject of Bel Canto, Lamperti also recommended the *messa di voce* as being the most satisfactory means of joining the register action. After the registers had been successfully joined, then he advised the practice of the *note filate*, which may be recognized as being similar to the *esclamazio languida*, in that the singer is required to swell from *pianissimo* to *forte* and then return.

The procedure advocated by Lamperti is made up of four stages of development. Of these the first is by far the longest. Tosi was also of the same opinion and made this very clear when, after stressing the importance of slow moving scales and pure intonation to the voice-building process, he said, 'the student now having made some remarkable progress, the instructor may acquaint him with the first embellishments of the art, which are the *appoggiaturas*.'

The opinion of Tosi and Lamperti was likewise shared by Mancini who declared, 'When a student has succeeded in fixing and sustaining his voice he may start on a cadenza, but it should be a short one.' First produce the voice correctly, build up each register until the normal power level has been reached, then begin to enter into more advanced stages of training. After 'remarkable' progress has been made, it is time to join the register action and so create the necessary conditions for the execution of embellishments requiring freedom and flexibility.

As soon as exercises assume a more extended form, *legato* singing becomes increasingly important. An interesting account of the development of a legato style is related by Johannes Hiller in *How to Teach Refined Singing* (1774). 'The essence of the so-called *legato*, or joining of notes,' he says, 'consists in there being no gap or pause in passing from one note to another, and no unpleasant slipping or dragging through smaller intervals. A beginner should sing an exercise first with only two slow notes, next with three, then with four. He must guard against any break in the joined sounds. Each succeeding note must follow so lightly and firmly as not to scoop, or show false intermediary sounds. This, too, not only on one syllable, or on one vowel, but on several. Also not only in scale passages, but in wider intervals upwards and downwards.'

The same principles that obtain in developing the less used, weaker register, may also be applied with equal success to the stronger. Here the *accentus* may be used or, if preferable, intervals of the major third or a full scale. After the student has attained a reasonable mastery and control over his technical resources the larger scale patterns may be used advantageously and, if the legato style is preserved, assure a perfect equalization of the scale, first within each register, later in negotiating the register crossing.

After each register has been separated and clearly defined there arises the necessity for interchanging the quality characteristics of each. This is essential because the two registers, if they are to ultimately fit together, must grow as they develop to be more alike, both as to quality and intensity.

As an aid to the mutation of the registers the interval of the octave will prove to be useful. The purpose of this exercise is to bring down as much of the falsetto as possible into the chest register. Thus, by starting in the falsetto at an appropriate place and carrying this register downward and adding it to the chest register an octave lower, some measure of co-ordinate action can be induced. Both male and female voices will benefit immeasurably by this exercise when it is properly executed. Another device having the same purpose is, of course, the *messa di voce*, or swelled tone on a single note.

FIGURE H

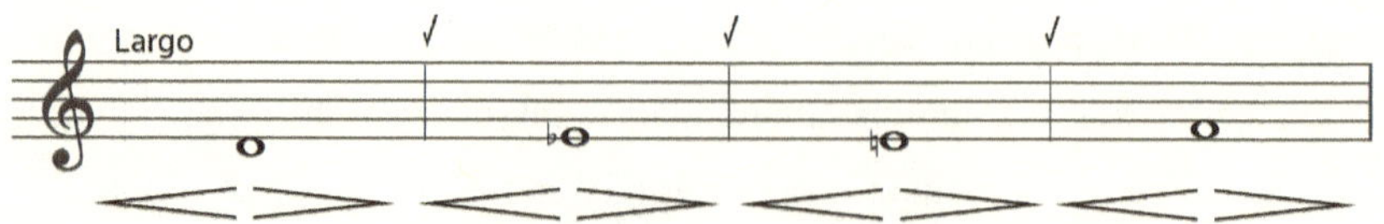

Fig. H. Showing the area of the register 'break' and the messa di voce.

FIGURE I

*Fig. I. Showing the change of register by means of the octave connection.
Upper tones are all falsetto, the lower ones belonging to the chest register.
This exercise tends to combine the quality characteristics of the two
registers and brings them more closely together. Notice how the octave
jump is merely a lower extenuation of the principle of the messa di voce,
i.e., to bring more falsetto into co-ordinate action with the chest register.*

Analysis of these exercises will show at a glance how the prime
purpose of each is likely to succeed. By *adding* the falsetto to the sturdy
chest register a greater measure of co-ordination is achieved. This
improvement is immediately reflected in the quality of the chest register
and, later, the falsetto. It is important to bear in mind, however, that neither
device should be used to bring the chest register up higher than F above
middle C, and only tenors and sopranos as high as that. To force the upward
extension of the chest register will seriously strain and possibly injure the
voice. *All tones* in all voices lying above F, lowest space of the treble staff,

properly belong to the falsetto, or 'feigned' voice, irrespective of the degree of volume employed.

When the singer has progressed into a classification that would include moderately difficult repertoire the simple turn may be taught, and this serves as an excellent preparatory exercise for the more taxing musical figures encountered in coloratura passages. These few exercises contain in themselves all the materials needed for the attainment of a complete technical mastery over the resources provided by the presence of the vocal registers. Changes are desirable to avoid monotony, but the guiding principles determining their selection should remain fixed.

'BUILDING ON THE SOFT'

For some time there has been in existence a school of thought subscribing to the theory that the voice is 'built on the soft.' This theory has been a direct outgrowth of the musical device the early Italians referred to as 'the art of producing the voice,' or the performance of the 'swelled tone,' the messa di voce.

Confused thinking has detracted from the usefulness of the original purpose of the *messa di voce*, however, in that all emphasis has been removed from the idea of 'building' and this school is now simply content to sing softly. No longer is any effort made to fulfill the original purpose of the *messa di voce*, which was to join the registers, and full-voiced singing is abhorred as injurious and inartistic.

In a correct performance of the exercise known as the *messa di voce* it is not enough just to start softly in an indiscriminate manner. A successful and beneficial performance of this device is only possible when the *proper kind of soft tone is used*. This means that the condition of the registration must be favorable. If once the idea of joining the co-ordinated falsetto, or 'feigned' voice, to the chest register has been lost the entire purpose of the exercise has been defeated.

The extent of the difference between 'building on the soft' and the *messa di voce* may be judged by the fact that the *messa di voce* was only practiced by students who were technically far advanced, whereas the practice of building on the soft voice is encouraged in mere beginners. The vocal abuse suffered by students whose attempts at learning to sing are confined to crooning is one of the tragedies of the profession. A properly produced soft tone is one of the major difficulties of vocal technique and can only be executed correctly after the registers are developed, balanced and perfectly united in their action.

Unless one is closely connected with the voice-teaching profession it is impossible to estimate the extent of the failure of many current methods of procedure. Only successful students of singing gain the attention of a wide public, and these are seldom successful in that they have been taught to sing but because they had naturally well-produced voices before training. The vast majority of vocal students fail abjectly in acquiring a sound technique of tone production. The fault is not their own but rests entirely with poor teaching practices. The consistent attempt to 'build on the soft' has been an imposing factor in determining the huge number of vocal failures.

Nearly victimized by having been subjected to this school of voice training was no less a figure than the late Enrico Caruso. His was an experience to make one think twice before risking the consequences involved in this practice. The story is now related in Caruso's own words and is included among other personal interviews in Harriette Brower's *Vocal Mastery*:

'I had always sung as far back as I can remember, for the pure love of it. My voice was contralto, and I sang in church in Naples from fourteen till

I was eighteen. Then I had to go into the army for awhile. I had never learned how to sing, for I had never been taught. One day a young officer of my company said to me, "You will spoil your voice if you keep on singing like that" — for I suppose I was fond of shouting in those days. "You must learn how to sing," he said to me, "you must study." He introduced me to a young man who at once took an interest in me and brought me to a singing master named Vergine. I sang for him, but he was very discouraging. His verdict was that it would be hopeless to try to make a singer out of me. As it was, I might possibly earn a few *lire* a night with my voice, but according to his idea I had far better stick to my father's trade, in which I could at least earn forty cents a day.

'But my young friend would not give up so easily. He begged Vergine to hear me again. Things went better with me the second time and Vergine consented to teach me.

'And now began a period of rigid discipline. In Vergine's idea I had been singing too loud. I must reverse this and sing everything softly. I felt as though in a straight-jacket, all my efforts at expression were carefully repressed; I was never allowed to let out my voice. At last came a chance to try my wings in opera, at ten *lire* a night ($2.00). In spite of the regime of repression to which I had been subjected for the past three years, there were still a few traces of my natural feeling left. The people were very Kind to me and I got a few engagements. Vergine had so long trained me to sing softly, never permitting me to sing out, that people began to call me "The Broken Tenor."

'A better chance came before long. In 1896 the Opera House in Salerno decided to produce *I Puritani*. At the last moment the tenor they had engaged to sing the leading role became ill. Lombardi, conductor of the orchestra, told the directors that there was a young singer in Naples, about eighteen miles away, who he knew could help out and sing the part. When they heard the name Caruso, they laughed scornfully. "What, the 'Broken

Tenor'?" they asked. But Lombardi pressed my claim, assured them I could be engaged, and no doubt would be glad to sing for nothing.

'So I was sent for. Lombardi talked with me awhile first. He explained by means of several illustrations that I must not stand cold and stiff in the middle of the stage, while I sang nice, sweet tones. No! I must let out my voice, I must throw myself into the part, I must be alive to it — and must live it and in it. In short, I must act as well as sing.

'It was all like a revelation to me. I had never realized before how absolutely necessary it was to act out the character I attempted. So I sang *I Puritani*, with as much success as could be expected of a young singer with so little experience. Something awoke in me at that moment. I was never called the "Broken Tenor" again. I made a regular engagement at two thousand lire a month. Out of this I regularly paid Vergine the 25% he always demanded.* He was somewhat reconciled to me when he saw that I had a real engagement and was making a substantial sum, though he insisted that I would lose my voice in a few years. But time passes on and I am still singing.' (4).

Twenty years to be exact, finally to be cut short at the height of his career because of death by pleurisy. During this time he was acclaimed as one of the greatest singers in the entire history of music.

This story of Caruso's early experience as a student and professional should surely highlight the dangers present in any misguided attempt to build the voice on the soft without making any effort to 'build,' or without understanding the Bel Canto procedure of blending the registers. Even more difficult to understand is the continued presence in the profession of teachers like Vergine who, when one who was potentially the greatest tenor the world of singing has perhaps known begs to be accepted as a pupil, turns him away and urges him to return to a trade to which his talents are

---

* This percentage payment out of income was the subject of later litigation. The judgment of the court invalidated Vergine's claim.

better fitted, namely, shoe cobbling. As if this crime were not enough, after three years of instruction this 'teacher' had succeeded in reducing this magnificent material to a status mockingly described as 'The Broken Tenor.' The hopeless incompetence of Vergine is further made evident when he predicted the early ruin of Caruso's voice because the tenor dared to sing full, ringing tones.

How many singers there must have been who, unlike Caruso, have not been so fortunate in discovering the magnitude of their errors in voice training until the damage was beyond all remedy. Never 'build on the soft' without first making certain that the registers are being joined and that the emphasis is actually being placed on 'building.' The practice can be a dangerous one! Tosi summed this situation up very nicely when he said, 'Experience shows that the piano is not to be trusted to, since it is prejudicial though pleasing; and if any one has a mind to lose his voice, let him try it.'

CHAPTER VIII

THE VIBRATO, TREMOLO AND WOBBLE

With the basic principles of a correct tone production now established, other considerations bearing upon beautiful singing assume ever-increasing importance. First among these are the propriety, usefulness and general classification of those voice movements commonly found a part of singing.

Early theoretical works dealing with the subject of vibratory pulsations present in every beautiful tone have been written by such eminent authorities as Mersenne of France and Simpson of England, both of whom lived in the seventeenth century, and the Italian Geminiani, an eighteenth-century theorist. Each of these historians, who were also outstanding musicians and performers, eulogized the expressive capacities and general merit of the vibrato in instrumental playing and demonstrated that the 'livening' of a tone by introducing a vibrato movement was a very early development of instrumental technique. Leopold Mozart, father of Wolfgang and one of the early masters of the violin, declared that 'Nature herself suggested it to man.' With regard to vocal performance there is evidence that the utility of the vibrato was a recognized and accepted phenomenon as early as the third century.

Voice movements, or periodic changes of pitch taking place during the sustaining of a single tone, fall into three general classes. First among these is a healthy, normal and efficient function called the 'vibrato.' The vibrato in singing serves the eminently useful purpose of giving life, vibrancy and buoyancy to a tone that would otherwise be 'dead.' Control over the vibrato, once it has been made a part of the technique by first having established the requisite conditions of registration and vowel purity, is maintained by the singer *indirectly* and is accomplished by regulating the intensity, or by simulating emotional effects.

Together with its variable and reflex response to changes of loudness and a strong tendency to vitalize the tone, the vibrato performs yet another useful function by enabling the singer to progress smoothly, freely and swiftly from tone to tone, in the manner of a glide (never a slur), to permit the singing of perfect legato passages. It was solely the perfection of the vibrato movement in the voices of the great Bel Canto artists that was directly accountable for the extreme feats of agility for which they were so justly famed. Without the vibrato all voices become awkward, cumbersome and inflexible, particularly when singing full voice.

To a considerable extent the condition of the vocal technique is measurable by the type of voice movement peculiar to the tone production at any given time. When the technique is undergoing an improvement there will be a simultaneous diminution of all faulty voice movements until finally a true vibrato gradually emerges. Conversely, when the technique is in a state of retrogression and disintegration, all traces of the vibrato will steadily disappear to be replaced, according to the nature of the faults being assimilated, by either the tremolo, the wobble, or a combination of the two.

It is impossible to overemphasize the fact that the vibrato is of inestimable importance to good singing, yet it must always be remembered that, like so many other phases of the vocal art, it cannot be regulated or controlled without injurious effect except by an indirect approach. *The vibrato must never be trained or cultivated!* All the teacher of singing, or the singer himself, may do is to observe its presence and the nature of its periodicity as a means of judging the efficiency of the vocal response. Only by applying the prime fundamentals of vocal technique, namely, by developing and balancing the registers properly and by centering the attention of the student on the production of tones of pure vowel quality, does it become possible to alter the character of the voice movement.

Whenever a feeling of hesitancy exists in the mind of the performer or listener as to the type and classification of voice movements the following rule may be applied to guide the ear: if one is *unaware* of any voice movement taking place, and the tone is 'alive,' resonant and vibrant, then it is certain that a vibrato action is present. Conversely, whenever there is a consciousness of a voice movement then that movement cannot be classified as a vibrato, but is a form of tremolo, wobble and the 'straight' tone, or some combination thereof. A correct vibrato action is inconspicuous, while all faulty movements are very noticeable.

The closest analogy to a correct vibrato movement may be studied in the performance of the violinist who, by shifting his finger position slightly above and below the mean pitch, causes a rapid oscillation to occur. As long as this pitch variation is the proper speed and not too wide a pitch change, the tone is quickened and made more vibrant. As with the singer, when the listener is unable to detect a pitch change the vibrato is being correctly executed. Should the attention be drawn at any time to noticeable changes of pitch, then the vibrato is being incorrectly performed, the quality becomes objectionable and the technique is faulty. In violin playing this is called an 'excessive vibrato.'

One of the essential differences between playing the violin and singing is that in vocal performance there is no such thing as having an 'excessive vibrato.' Any voice movement in singing suitably described 'excessive,' whether it be too rapid and fluttery, or too slow and wobbly, stems from an entirely different arrangement and co-ordination of the voice parts and bears no relationship to the vibrato either as to cause or effect. Whereas the vibrato is always the result of a correctly functioning mechanism, the tremolo usually denotes the presence of throatiness, while the wobbly and unsteady tone shows that the instrument is being unduly strained and overburdened by forcing for volume. Persistent indulgence in either the tremolo or the wobble inevitably leads to a complete loss of voice, but the continued presence of the vibrato is assurance of a soundness of technique guaranteeing its preservation.

To trace the origin and find the cause of the vibrato, tremolo and wobble, it becomes necessary to establish the mechanical principles of tone production resulting in a voice movement, or pitch fluctuation. By so doing, it will be discovered that the operation of these movements as a psychological response of the voice parts involves, directly or indirectly, the entire organization of the vocal mechanism.

Human beings are able to sing and speak because of the vocal organs, a mechanism comprised of a voice box, more properly called the *larynx*, situated in the throat. Within the larynx itself two bands of flesh are suspended. These are the vocal cords, which are securely fastened and held along their lateral sides and at their ends by a complicated arrangement of muscles whose contraction brings them into tension as they resist the pressure of the breath directed against them. The tension thus created causes the vocal cords to vibrate, the degree of tension being proportionate to the speed of the vibration which in turn is responsible for the position of the pitch in the musical scale.

When in a position of rest the two vocal bands meet and are joined at their front ends, but separate as they approach the opposite side of the larynx so that the outline of their position in repose is that of the inverted Roman numeral five.

In singing, the two ends of the vocal cords that are separated are drawn together by the action of the arytenoid cartilages. These cartilages rotate, closing the opening to the passage of the breath and causing the vocal cords to adjust so that their edges run parallel to one another. In this way the glottal opening, or the air space between the vocal cords, is narrowed.

Once the cords have been brought together and held in position against the expiratory pressure of the breath by tension of the cricoid and arytenoid muscles, they become activated and are set into vibration. The speed at which they vibrate establishes pitch, and when the resonance cavities have been adjusted to amplify the tone and form the vowel the vocal organs become a musical instrument.

After the pressure of the breath against the stretched vocal cords has set them into vibration an unusual action occurs. Instead of remaining in a fixed position of vibratory tension the cords yield somewhat to the breath pressure exerted beneath them so that the air escaping from the lungs is released in a series of puffs. With each puff the cords spread apart momentarily; then, after the briefest interruption the opening immediately closes as the cords in an undulating motion return to normal position. This action occurs and re-occurs constantly throughout singing and oscillagraph tracings show that each undulation is completed slightly more than six times each second.

The bowing action performed by the vocal cords as they yield to the pressure of the breath is similar in many respects to the action of any elastic matter that is stretched and, following a reduction of pressure, reacts by springing back to its original position. With the vocal cords the upward and outward movement followed causes a slight raising of the pitch to take place. With the reduction of breath pressure made possible by the escape of each puff of air this change is straightway counteracted by a lowering of the pitch while the vocal cords spring back to their normal position. During this return to normal position the mean pitch is exceeded so that when a tone is sustained a series of rapid pitch fluctuations take place whereby the tone that is heard actually represents the center point of a rapid alteration between an imperceptibly raised peak and a slightly lowered depression. One of the most important features of this phenomenon is the *regularity* of its occurence, both in amplitude, that is to say, in width of pitch change, and in periodicity, or the number of oscillations per second.

The action just described is heard in singing as a vibrato. So far the discussion has dealt primarily with the movement of the vocal cords, the fact that this movement causes a pitch change, and the effect of the pitch change on the audible qualities of the tone itself. Of greater interest, but lesser importance because of the absence of any means whereby the singer may gain direct control over their function, is knowing the exact muscular contractions that take place when the conditions essential to a vibrato have been established.

It is difficult, if not impossible, to describe with fidelity the complicated muscular contractions necessary to produce a vibrato. So complex is the interplay between the various segments involved that even anatomists disagree. Besides, it is extremely doubtful if any purpose useful to producing better tone quality in singing would be served, inasmuch as these muscular functions are not subject to volitional control. Suffice it to say, therefore, that it is reasonable to assume that a certain specific arrangement of these muscular contractions is favorable to the production of a vibrato while other arrangements, or co-ordinations, are not. Furthermore, it may also be assumed that when the contractions of the muscles involved in phonation are not working harmoniously and co-operatively, the conditions necessary to produce a vibrato action have been destroyed. When this happens the vibrato disappears and is replaced by another type of voice movement less favorable to beautiful singing and reflecting the degree of disunity within the mechanism itself. Thus, apart from the vibrato, there is the tremolo and wobble.

When the vocal mechanism is co-ordinating effectively, one of the outstanding features of the technique is the regularity of the vibrato pulsations. With the appearance of false tensions arising from muscular interference, however, this change in the harmonious arrangement of the voice parts is immediately reflected in the character of the sounds produced. In place of the even and regularly occurring pulsation of the vibrato, irregular pulsations are heard. These alter the quality of the tone and offend the discriminating ear.

The offensiveness of the tremolo and wobble as an aesthetic consideration is much less important to the present context than the fact that these pulsations are caused by muscular interference. It is wrong, therefore, not to distinguish between the various types of voice movement and relate each to a separate causation. Failure to recognize and distinguish the vibrato from its opposites only leads to an acceptance of tone qualities and habits of singing that are in themselves responsible for the continuance of the tremolo and wobble.

Once faulty voice movements are recognized as being due to muscular interference, then the necessary corrective measures will be sought and used to remedy the situation. Apart from the voice movement itself the extent of the muscular interference inhibiting the performer may be judged by the extent of the limitations imposed. These limitations may be appraised by observing the ease or difficulty with which long musical phrases are negotiated, and by the singer's ability to sing high and low, loudly and softly, and to swell and diminish with freedom. Correction of the vocal faults caused by muscular interference is made by purifying the vowel quality, and by bringing the registers into proper balance and alignment.

Although the early masters of Bel Canto never addressed themselves to problems dealing with the function of the anatomical parts of the vocal mechanism, they were well aware of the relationship of tone quality to physiological causes. Beauty and steadiness of tone were considered the very foundation of a sound singing technique. Firm tones of lovely quality are only produced as the result of a congenial arrangement and effective co-ordination of the vocal organs.

The present confused state of opinion concerning the status of voice movements as related to the vocal style of Bel Canto have evolved mainly from statements made by leading teachers of that era in reference to the subject. In essence, this opinion has been summarized by Tenducci who said, 'the first and most necessary rule in singing is to keep the voice steady.'

At first glance the impression received from this instruction is that a complete absence of all voice movement is desirable, and it is this somewhat hastily formed opinion that persists to the present. But 'steady,' rather than denoting the absence of movement in all vocal tone, in reality implies a *consistency* and regularity of pulsation that is a most admirable concomitant of good vocalization. A steady tone, of a kind that admits no pitch variation whatever, is not only ugly but cumbersome and lifeless. This kind of tone production hardly answers the description of the singing style of the Bel Canto performer.

The merits of a style of tone production that avoids any kind of pitch variation may easily be weighed by the simple expedient of experimenting with tones answering that description and analyzing the result. In the first place, not even a poorly used voice will find this such an easy thing to do, while voices of really good quality will find it almost impossible. The initial impression gained from such an experiment is that the process is an unnatural one and subjects the throat to constant strain and excessive effort.

To carry this experiment further and attempt to sing rapid scale passages reveals other glaring weaknesses in the procedure. Intonation that is under normal conditions perfect suddenly becomes ill-defined. The voice quality itself is suddenly transformed from a buoyant, youthful sound to a tired, worn quality, and the entire apparatus becomes unmanageable and unresponsive to the demands of flexibility. Tempos tend to drag and persistent trials reveal that the voice not only suffers in quality but also fatigues with extreme rapidity. It is utterly impossible that the wonderful lyricism of the Bel Canto singers' voices could ever have evolved out of such a procedure.

Despite the fact that most of the theoretical writings of the early teachers refers to the desirability of having 'steadiness' of tone, there is ample evidence to prove that their intention and meaning was to denote regularity and consistency of movement rather than an absence of all pulsation. A proper voice movement, or vibrato, was doubtless thought to be 'steady,' mainly because it is unobtrusive, and the pitch change so regular and even that no sense of oscillation could be gained.

A scholarly work by W. J. Henderson, *The Early History of Singing*, refutes many opinions currently entertained on the subject of voice movements in the singing techniques of preceding centuries. In this work Henderson discusses the types of voice movement found acceptable and appropriate to the singing of chants even in the very earliest days of church music.

The source of Henderson's information was derived from the distinguished biographer of Palestrina, Baini (1775-1844). From manuscript letters found at Rheims, Metz and Soissons, written by Vatican authorities to Pepin and Charlemagne, it was discovered that the singers of the earliest period of musical history not only had at their command the equivalent of our vibrato but also were able to produce at will many variations of this voice movement as a means of creating artistic and emotional effects.

The principal expressive devices used in the early days of the Christian era may be summarized as follows: (1) the *crispatio*, (2) *trepidatio*, (3) *reverberatio*, (4) *vinnulae*, and (5) *voces tremulae*.

That these voice movements, together with the pure vibrato, were looked upon as tonal fluctuations may be deduced from the definition provided by Pomponius Festus, a grammarian of the third century who wrote, '*Vibrissare est vocem in cantando crispare*.' Translated this means, 'The vibrato is a singing style where the voice shakes backward and forward.'

The extent of the expressive capacities of the numerous fluctuations outlined above shows that the singers of the Bel Canto era possessed vocal techniques permitting the performer to produce any one of a number of voice movements at will. Unfortunately, the precise indication and meaning of the terms employed to describe the expressive and interpretive uses of the vibrato is lacking and one may only guess at the full significance implied. What has been shown, however, is the fact that there was a general recognition and acceptance of the vibrato as an artistic medium at a time long thought of as having been hostile to its use.

In defining the terms used to describe the different classifications of voice movement in singing, it is discovered that each expression is rooted in an emotional context suitable and common to artistic expression and interpretive effect. The *trepidatio* was a term indicating a tremble, or shake, perhaps the shaking and trembling normally associated with fear. *Reverberatio* is a derivative of medieval Latin rather than the classic, and signifies a throbbing quality in singing such as is produced when the fullest resonance of the voice is employed.

The opposite of the *reverberatio* was the *vinnulae*, meaning 'sweet.' Here a different type of voice movement is required and the full resonance of the *reverberatio* was replaced by a movement more in keeping with the quiet atmosphere created by a finely spun *pianissimo*. *Voces tremulae*, of course, could only signify a trembling effect, but just how this differs from the *trepidatio* is not known. The *crispatio* is the pure vibrato as it operates in normal, or melodic, singing when the tone production is correct. If it were in any way possible to reconstruct an exact picture of the way these voice movements were used as interpretive effects, greater insight would be provided into the musical as well as the vocal style of Bel Canto.

Insofar as research into the subject matter related to voice movements is concerned, nothing is revealed to indicate that there might have been undesirable aspects of tonal fluctuations until comparatively recent times. Statements such as 'keep the voice steady,' it is true, seem to include by inference the fact that not all voices of the time were blessed with this faculty. Tosi warned against the 'trembling of the voice,' but evidently felt that the condition as it prevailed in his day was not sufficiently serious to warrant more than superficial comment. Not until the publication of Francesco Lamperti's *A Treatise on the Art of Singing* (1818) is it made clear that strongly distasteful elements of tonal movement were often present in tone production and that these faults must be remedied if the voice is to become beautiful.

Lamperti's treatise deals with the problem of the vibrato versus the tremolo forthrightly by saying, 'I will put the pupil on his guard against the trembling of the voice which is sufficient to exclude the singer from the stage. I will not have him, however, confound this with the oscillation produced by the expression of an impassioned sentiment.' Obviously, this statement proves that at least two types of voice movement were recognized at this period. As one was sought after and the other rejected there must have been an essential difference between them as to kind and cause.

The dearth of material so evident in the writings of the early teachers of Bel Canto concerning the types of voice movement can be accepted as evidence that unsteadiness of voice was not one of the problems with which they were often called upon to dispose. In all probability such difficulties were known to resolve themselves by merely purifying the vowel qualities produced and by improving the balance and development of the registers. In any event, this has been the author's experience. It is also more than probable that the omnipresence of the tremolo and wobble in singing today is the direct result of teaching procedures wholly at variance with the principles of Bel Canto. Rarely does one hear an untrained singer, provided he is free of the nervous tension aroused by unaccustomed public performance, whose voice is troubled by either the wobble or the tremolo. There is every reason to believe that only *after* training do these unpleasant voice movements become a part of the singer's vocal equipment.

Little doubt should remain in the minds of either the theorists or the practitioners of the art of singing that some form of voice pulsation is necessary to sing effectively. What is needed, however, is a general clarification of the position of the various types of movement in that relationship. Too much confusion still exists as to the desirable as opposed to the undesirable qualities of pulsation, and there is too great an inclination to unite the causation of the different movements under a single heading. Thus, one; hears such anachronisms as 'excessive vibrato' used to describe a wobble, or one will hear the tremolo spoken of to mean a vibrato, etc. The extent of the confusion may be judged when a scientific investigator of the status of Carl Seashore publishes the results of his laboratory experiments (*Psychology of Music*) and refers to 'good vibratos' and 'bad vibratos.' Of course, there is no such thing as having a 'bad vibrato,' and the term is self-contradictory.

Three noteworthy features belong exclusively to the vibrato. First and foremost is the *regularity* of its periodicity as opposed to the *irregularity* of pulsation always found with the tremolo and wobble. Regardless of the loudness being sung the vibrato cycle is completed about six and one-half times each second with absolute consistency. On the other hand, the tremolo will often pulsate more than eight times a second, while the wobble will move as slowly as four. Equally important is the fact that these cycles are not constant and vary considerably with changes of intensity. Briefly stated, the reaction of the tremolo and wobble to variations of loudness is to show a marked change in periodicity, but not in amplitude, whereas the vibrato will change in amplitude, but not in periodicity.

The reaction of the tremolo and wobble to changes of loudness is additional and conclusive proof of their being functions of the mechanism quite separate and apart from the vibrato. The only response made by the vibrato to changes of intensity is by an increase or decrease in amplitude, *not in the speed of the vibrato cycle itself.* Two factors alone govern the amplitude of the vibrato. One of these is pitch, the other is loudness.

For every tone in the vocal range there is an ideal amplitude of the vibrato. This amplitude has its equivalent expression in loudness, or volume. Thus, when increasing and decreasing the volume of tone produced, the amplitude of the vibrato adjusts itself correspondingly. At pianissimo the amplitude is reduced to almost zero, while at fortissimo a pitch change of approximately a semi-tone takes place. Through all stages of intermediary loudness a perfect gradation of amplitude performs the transition from one extreme to the other. The swelling of a single tone without forcing, therefore, is accomplished by an increase in the amplitude of the vibrato. This action, of course, takes place reflexly when the singer performs the *messa di voce* after the registration is properly balanced.

Pitch is one of the governing factors determining the amplitude of the vibrato by reason of the fact that the voice shows an inclination, even when the intensity is held constant, to narrow the pitch change slightly as the scale is descended. In the lower octave of the voice there is relatively little fluctuation even when singing full voice. There is, therefore, much greater opportunity for increasing and decreasing the intensity in the upper portion of the voice, and for creating a much wider variety of emotional expression, than is possible in the lower area. Composers who write well for the voice always take this into consideration.

The second feature of the vibrato is that the slight pitch variation natural to it creates a pulsation directly responsible for a flexible tone production. When the early masters of Bel Canto refused to cultivate agility and flexibility during the early stages of voice training, it was because they knew that flexibility is vocally impossible until such time as the voice has been adequately prepared and conditioned to cope with the task.

Vocal flexibility and the ability to run scales smoothly, rapidly and accurately are determined solely on the basis of whether or not the singer has set up those conditions of purity of intonation within a balanced registration which alone leads to the acquisition of a true vibrato. To attempt to cultivate flexibility before the conditions have been made right is futile. Vocal agility will come, after proper training, very gradually as a *result* of improved conditions within the vocal mechanism. Once a natural vibrato appears, then the voice moves with ease and freedom, swiftly and surely, through its wide range.

The third feature of the vibrato is found in its contribution to ease in singing. To stand still, completely motionless, for any length of time is considerably more difficult and fatiguing than it is to move freely. The opposed muscular system responsible for a condition of body 'tone' demands a constant release and pickup of tension to avoid tiring. Engineers acknowledge this principle when constructing a large bridge or building by making allowance for sway and 'give' in order to eliminate the strain engendered by absolute rigidity. When Leopold Mozart declared of the vibrato that 'Nature herself suggested it to man,' he arrived at the very essence of the phenomenon. For just as the vibrato is 'natural' to beautiful tone so, too, is flexibility and ease of execution natural to the vibrator.

The voice having a correct vibrato movement is not only freely produced and therefore flexible, but is also able to establish changes of pitch with exactness and precision. When the voice moves on a vibrato pulsation there can be no slurring through intermediary tones during the performance of scales and passages. Whether the interval be large or small, each tone is clearly defined both as to quality, pitch and duration. Slurring, apart from being inartistic and unmusical, further demonstrates that the muscular co-ordination of the vocal organs is faulty and unresponsive to the demands of the singer.

Attempts are sometimes made to avoid slurring without first setting up those conditions leading to the acquisition of a true vibrato by detaching the tones comprising the musical phrase. This practice is not be to condoned as it only substitutes one vocal fault for another, and 'jerking' from tone to tone is equally damaging to the technique as it is unmusical. In each case the tone production is an example of an improper muscular coordination whose correction depends upon realigning the balance within the registration and purification of the vowel quality. No other solution is satisfactory, and any other approach a subterfuge which is at best superficial.

The substance of the conclusions to be drawn from observing the presence of vibratory impulses in singing, therefore, is as follows. All voices should have a vibrato, which is conducive to ease in singing and which plays an active part as an interpretive device, both as to regulating the intensity and altering the expression of mood and feeling. In developing the voice, absolutely no effort should ever be made to interfere with the type of voice movement of whatever kind. When the voice movement is faulty, then the fault is due to mechanical imperfections, most common among them being an improperly balanced and developed registration and the inevitable vowel distortions occasioned by 'throatiness,' or other tonal blemishes. Once these *causes* have been removed the voice movement will *readjust itself*. The vibrato will appear and the way made open for artistic singing.

After the vibrato has been securely made a part of the technique it first becomes possible for the singer to gain a substantial control over its action and produce by artistic means any emotional effects such as habitually disturb the steadiness of the voice. Fear, anger, joy, etc., all have their equivalent type of voice movement falling well within the expressive capacity of the vibrato. But it must always be remembered that the safest way to command a correct response of the vibrato mechanism is for the singer to evoke the emotion he is seeking to portray and allow natural processes to reveal the emotion he genuinely feels. The performer whose voice works well, and who has the intellectual and emotional depth to revivify the import of the text, may then reach the goal toward which all vocal study should be directed and become the vocal artist.

THE TREMOLO

In order to distinguish the tremolo from the vibrato it only becomes necessary to contemplate the peculiarities of the voice movement that give offense. Because the vibrato maintains a pitch fluctuation of constant speed and periodicity the listener is always impressed by a sense of beauty, ease, security, and resonance. The rhythmic pitch change taking place with absolute regularity is entirely inconspicuous. As the tremolo does not possess these qualities, and because its pulsation is too rapid, as well as deficient in amplitude, the listener is quickly and unpleasantly conscious of its motion.

The physiological cause of the tremolo is in no way related to the vibrato, and the two owe their being to separate modes of tone production. All evidence indicates that the tremolo is the result of a throaty tone production.

Throatiness is the most deplorable of all vocal habits and is developed by the gradual acquisition of a technique of tone production that is reverse to the natural and intended function of the vocal organs. Instead of the extensor muscles coming into action to allow the free passage of tone the throaty singer activates constrictor tensions. These tensions cause a distortion of the tone quality and reduce the efficiency of the vocal response. The characteristic quality that has long been associated with a constriction is described as 'throaty.'

Throaty singing may be of two kinds. The first is a strong and active constriction brought on by vigorous singing; the second is less easily detectable, yet more insidious, because the tension is disguised by singing lightly in the half-voice. In both instances, however, the technique is the same, the principal difference being one of degree.

The strain engendered by throatiness is, of course, unnatural. In order to avoid discomfort the vocal organs seek for relief by distributing the tension over as wide an area of surrounding musculature as possible. For this reason the tension created by the throaty singer, irrespective of its mildness or aggressiveness, spreads to the muscles of the jaw and tongue and does not remain confined to the throat itself. With the continuance of throaty singing, the tension built up causes a fluttering of the entire mechanism. It is this fluttering on a constrictor tension that is heard in the tone as a tremolo. Closer study usually betrays the presence of a tongue and jaw movement which synchronizes perfectly with the tonal flutter.

When the technique is one that produces a tremolo nothing will remain of the vibrato until a complete change-about and restoration of the tone production has been effected. Being opposite extremes of muscular co-ordination, the tremolo and vibrato are antipathetic and cannot exist together. It is therefore correct to think of the vibrato as a healthful muscular coordination, just as it is correct to consider the tremolo in terms of muscular interference.

The tremolo, then, is the result of friction arising from an improper muscular co-ordination. Muscles that should be relaxed during singing become active, while those that should be active remain passive. This absence of stability between antagonistic groups of laryngeal muscles is responsible for a majority of the difficulties encountered in singing. The throat, instead of being free and pliable, becomes stiff and awkward, and the singer experiences unbelievable difficulty, finding it an almost insuperable problem to establish a condition of resonance, or to move from note to note freely and in tune.

Conditions of throat tension growing out of the tremolo are not only extended to include the jaw and tongue, but apparently affect the functioning of the ear itself. Many of the singers presently appearing before the public sing badly out of tune, yet none are deficient in pitch perception. This is because the condition of throat tension interferes with and prohibits the accurate adjustment of the voice parts as they move in response to the mental impetus.

Before sounding a note of any definite pitch and quality the singer must first have a mental impression of the sound he is desirous of producing. The specific makeup of this concept has to do with pitch, duration, vowel quality and intensity. In singing a song the problem becomes more complex because conditions are constantly changing. The pitch and duration vary, innumerable vowels and consonants may be introduced, and the intensities often include every gradation from very soft to very loud. In such instances the mental concept must be broadened to include complete musical phrases. Each musical phrase should be heard mentally in its entirety *before* the first note is sung.

Artistic interpretation is to a large degree dependent upon the skill of the performer in perceiving the relationship of one musical phrase to another, and on his ability to balance all the parts making up the entire composition with taste and discrimination. In this way the song or aria is unified by thought processes, translated into musical phrases, that flow logically one upon the other. It is solely due to an imperfect physical response to mental stimuli, i.e., faulty technique, that causes a difference between the pitch or phrase that is heard mentally, and the sounds that are actually produced.

Intonation, therefore, is solely dependent upon two factors. First, the ability on the part of the performer to mentally hear the tone, or tones, that are to be sung and, second, the physical ability to translate the mental image into reality. The effect of a constrictor tension in the form of the tremolo very often upsets the accuracy of the mechanical response and the result is off-pitch singing. This condition is almost always due to an imperfect muscular co-ordination of the vocal mechanism itself, seldom to hazy mental concepts. Whenever a student cannot *mentally* distinguish pitch he should be dissuaded from engaging in further study.

The cure for the tremolo evolves from the same logic that should be applied to remedy any other vocal fault, namely, that the quality of sound being produced is fundamentally wrong and represents an incorrect functioning of the vocal mechanism. The first obligation of the teacher in such instances is to immediately proceed to the problem of the registers and re-establish them in their divided form, with the closest attention being given at all times to the purity of the vowel quality. By this procedure alone the first major step toward a complete realignment of the muscular co-ordination will have been made.

Once each register has been made to respond in its natural manner, the tone quality will change and all evidence of the tremolo will gradually disappear. Intonation is improved and the production freer and easier. Invariably a simultaneous phase of the progress made will include a noticeable extension of the voice range and a considerable increase in power and resonance. By deliberately relaxing the muscles of the neck, chest, shoulders, tongue and jaw, the voice soon learns to respond quickly and efficiently to the mental image. With these conditions established there will no longer be justification for a tonal flutter and the tremolo is forever eliminated from the technique.

THE WOBBLE

As its name suggests, the wobble heard in singing is a pitch change whose width and unevenness of amplitude and periodicity are its distinguishing features. Like the tremolo, but unlike the vibrato, there is no relationship between the amplitude of the pitch change that takes place in the wobbly tone and the intensity of the sound produced.

The wobble differs from both the tremolo and the vibrato in very important respects and, of course, is due to a physiological cause quite separate and apart from those responsible for the other voice movements. Where the vibrato is a perfectly even pulsation whose amplitude is governed by intensity, and the tremolo an irregular tonal flutter whose origins may be traced to a constriction, the wobbly tone is a slow, wide pitch change which is caused by 'driving' and forcing the voice. Basses and contraltos frequently bring to their singing those qualities of tone production causing a wobble, and the 'thick,' clumsy, heavy quality so often heard in low voices, in every respect forced, unnatural and 'put on,' attests to the unsoundness of this singing style.

The singer possessing a vocal technique inclining toward the wobble is, however, technically much better off than the singer afflicted by the tremolo. Both voice types are the result of an incorrect way of singing but, whereas the tremolo is the result of a constriction, the wobbly tone is relatively free, being entirely due to forcing the registers beyond their natural boundaries. By simply reducing the upward drive and 'push,' and re-establishing the registers and bringing them into proper balance, this condition is relieved very quickly. The fact that a majority of those who sing Grand Opera are victims of the wobble is sufficient evidence to prove that this kind of voice movement, while distressing to hear, is nevertheless more closely allied to a healthful function of the vocal organs than the tremolo. Seldom is the voice suffering from a tremolo able to withstand the rigors of an operatic season, unless confined to singing minor roles.

Correction of the wobble is a very simple process. As forcing for volume is usually the cause the first step is to reduce the energy expended so that all 'push' is eliminated. A sense of 'hold' must be developed (not to be confused with a 'grip' or squeeze), rather than 'drive.' Furthermore, as forcing always tends to weaken the power level of the lower tones, the attention of the teacher must be directed toward developing this area of the voice and bringing it once again into proper balance with the normal resonance of the upper middle range. This often necessitates holding back the energy expended in the production of the upper middle tones. When this has been done the high tones will immediately benefit and the whole intensity scale of the voice will become much more smooth and even.

The second and even more important step in eliminating the wobble is promptly to give the male falsetto and the female chest register the prominence in the technique to which they are justly entitled. The chest register must not be used higher than the bottom line of the treble staff for any voice, male or female. With the chest register thus confined within its natural limits the falsetto must be brought into continually greater prominence and worked *down* into the chest register and made to co-ordinate with it. This process enriches the quality, power and vibrancy of the chest register and eases the burden imposed by using the chest register alone.

Artistic singing is so completely dependent upon the performer being free to express himself the way he *wants* to, rather than the way he *has* to, the fact is self-evident that avoidance of the dangers and limitations inherent in the tremolo and wobble is imperative. Only when the voice works freely, permitting a vibrato to appear, is the vocalist able to shape and control a beautiful melodic line. Mastery of the basic principles of a Bel Canto technique alone assures the performer of having at his command the resources of a true vibrato.

CHAPTER IX

BREATHING

Perhaps no single phase of singing has been made the subject of such extended discussion and debate as the proper manner of breathing. A vast literature has sprung up devoted to the wonders of 'breath control' and many essentially contradictory theories have been advanced.

Although a few writers have thoroughly disproved the plausibility of all theories directed toward control of the breath, notably David C. Taylor and Sir Charles Bell, and proved conclusively that it is a physical impossibility to regulate the rate of breath expulsion, nevertheless this phase of instruction remains the basis of almost every modern school of instruction.

Many important objections present themselves by way of protest against the exaggerated stress placed upon the importance of breathing, to the neglect of other and more fundamental problems. There has never been even a suspicion of proof that mastery of singing is in any way dependent upon a correct system of breathing. Quite the contrary: as each of the three systems of breathing can be mastered by students of no more than average intelligence and ability within a very short time, the evidence compels one to accept precisely the opposite conclusion, namely, that the manner of breathing is largely without influence in determining the efficiency of the vocal technique.

Other arguments readily disprove the hastily formed and illogical conclusion of those who agree with Maria Celioni who said, 'He who knows how to breathe, knows how to sing.' The entire history of singing is replete with examples of singers who have at one time had beautiful voices, only to lose them prematurely. Could it be that these people were so incredibly stupid as to forget the proper manner of breathing after once having mastered it? Of course not! The world today is full of singers whose respiration in singing is managed perfectly. But are they perfect singers? Obviously not! Yet perfection always equals perfection and the perfectly working vocal mechanism always produces the perfect tone. Therefore, while it is true that there are good and bad methods of breathing, and a correct and an incorrect way to perform the act, no *transformation* of the vocal technique itself is effected by the employment of either one means as against the other. It would be much closer to the truth to say that when the vocal mechanism is working efficiently very little is demanded of the breath, *because all of the energy used in singing is being directed into constructive channels*. Therefore, as the breath is not dissipated and wasted the singer discovers that he has more at his disposal than his needs require.

The earliest theoretical writings on voice support this contention and the subject of breathing is treated with almost complete indifference. Caccini mentions it in a casual way, but neither Tosi nor Mancini discuss it at all. The typical attitude of the early teachers is perhaps summed up with charming naiveté by Ferrari in *A Concise Treatise on Italian Singing*, who advises that 'the inspiration should be made at the beginning and at the end of the musical phrase.'

An equally amusing story is recounted concerning one Vincenzo Cirillo, a pupil of Mercadante. When asked by one of his own students how to breathe, he exclaimed, '*Mio Dio*, if God has not taught you how to breathe it is time you were buried!'

The inference is plain throughout the available literature on the subject of breathing by authoritative instructors of the seventeenth and eighteenth centuries that the almost total absence of this topic from their published accounts was deliberate. It is impossible to believe that an oversight was committed and the only conclusion to be drawn is that the respiratory processes were known to instinctively fall into line once the fundamental principles of tone production had been established. In comparison to the problems of registration and purity of tone quality it is apparent the subject of breathing merited no more than a place of minor importance in Bel Canto instruction.

For some time it has been the author's experience, in working out the principles of Bel Canto in his own teaching, that once the student has been made to breathe without raising his chest or shoulders the taking of a breath will automatically cause the diaphragm to do the work for which it was intended by nature. By keeping the chest and shoulders quiet they are unable to come into tension and interfere with the neck muscles. Because of the continued relaxation of the neck muscles the vocal organs are left free to establish pitch and resonate the vowels without hindrance. As a result the tones issue forth with complete freedom and clarity. Because it is produced with greater freedom, the voice is not only purer in quality but consumes only a fraction of the energy provided by the quantity of breath originally inspired.

Of three possible techniques of breathing, one is the least desirable and must be avoided at all costs. This is called clavicular, or scapula, breathing.

Clavicular breathing is a system of inspiration whereby the upper parts of the chest are raised while the diaphragm is drawn in. The effect of this method of breathing is first to interfere with, and then destroy, the effective co-ordination of the vocal organs.

Two important reasons make clavicular breathing useless as a practical technique. First of these is that by raising the chest and lifting the shoulders the muscles of the neck are brought into tension. This constitutes an unnecessary involvement and the tension of the neck muscles soon spreads until the entire upper portion of the anatomy becomes rigidly inflexible. All sense of tonal 'support,' body poise and control is speedily lost and, wanting this, the voice 'grips' instead of 'holds' and the technique gradually becomes throaty.

The lesser penalty for singing with a high chest position is that only a partial inspiration can be completed. As the diaphragm is dome-shaped, the act of drawing the diaphragm upward and raising the chest means that only a fraction of its capacity for storing energy is utilized. All the lower air spaces having the greatest area for expansion are deliberately shut off and reduced to a mere fraction of their potential. At the same time the smaller region at the top is crammed beyond all reason. This is the kind of breathing that leads to early fatigue of the vocal organs and a premature decline in the vocal powers of all those addicted to this practice.

Another unfortunate habit of breathing sometimes employed in singing is taking the breath through the nose with the mouth tightly closed. The practice of this fanciful notion is one of the newer developments in voice-training methods and its invention probably has been necessitated by the increasing prevalence, since the turn of the century, of unnatural habits of tone production. As a practical consideration breathing through the nose is inefficient because (1) it is stilted and awkward, (2) it prohibits the swift and quiet inhalation of requisite amounts of air, and (3) it is inclined to lead to a high chest position, which in turn induces throatiness.

Whenever the voice has been subjected to strain, it is Nature's way to soothe the irritation set up by creating greater quantities of saliva. Continued irritation will soon dry up the source of supply, however, and the singer becomes increasingly aware of an unpleasant parchness of the throat. Persistent efforts to continue singing lead to an aggravation of the condition which can only be cured by a period of rest, followed-by constructive vocal study. Incipient stages of throat dryness, it is true, may sometimes be relieved to a certain extent through warming the air by having it pass through the nose instead of the mouth, but no *cure* for the condition causing throat dryness could possibly be effected in this way as the cause has not been removed. Normally a dry throat is Nature's first warning that all is not well with the vocal organs, and it is the better part of wisdom for the singer to heed the warning promptly by adopting a new technique of singing.

From a standpoint of artistic usage the procedure of breathing through the nose is too ludicrous for comment. Imagine a rendition of the *Largo al factotum*, or the Nightmare Song from *lolanthe*, as it would sound when performed by a singer who breathed through the nose!

Of the two remaining and infinitely preferable techniques of breathing, the first is called *diaphragmatic*, or abdominal. Sometimes the taking of the breath into the body by expanding the lower area of the lungs, or abdominal space, is also spoken of as 'costal' breathing.

Costal breathing is universally practiced for purposes of daily living. Throughout the completion of the cycle of inspiration and expiration the chest remains passive and the lower ribs are without perceptible movement. A noteworthy feature of this style of breathing is the slight protrusion of the stomach with every inspiration.

For purposes of singing, costal breathing is normal as long as the musical expression does not include dramatic episodes, or phrases to be sung *con grande expansione*. For as soon as passages demanding great breath of style are encountered the diaphragmatic method is deficient and the breathing apparatus, expanding to utilize all its resources, receives assistance through an outward movement of the lower ribs. This movement fills the lungs to their fullest capacity and the breath taken in this manner may be described as *thoracic*, or *intercostal* breathing. The effect of intercostal breathing is to create a feeling of expansion around the entire middle part of the body, so that the expansion will include the small of the back and sides, as well as the abdominal wall. It is imperative at all times for the chest and shoulders to remain quiet and relaxed throughout both costal and intercostal breathing, otherwise the tension of the diaphragm will be released and shift upward.

BREATH 'CONTROL'

The expression 'breath control' is one of the most frequently used and most maligned phrases in the entire jargon of the voice-teaching profession. If it is meant by 'breath control' that the singer adopts a systematic way of breathing during singing, then the expression is harmless. But, more often than not, 'breath control' refers to a technique of breathing whereby the rate of the escaping breath is checked and regulated in order to facilitate the negotiation of long musical phrases.

Almost without exception the efficiency of the vocal mechanism may be judged by the natural rate of the uncontrolled breath expulsion. The well-produced voice always seems to have more breath in reserve even after having sung consecutive phrases of inordinate length and difficulty, while the poorly used voice forever seems to be gasping and in obvious distress. This difference, of course, is not due to a voluntarily controlled emission, but is entirely the result of a well-balanced registration. Muscular contractions determining the ratio of registration are directly responsible for the success or failure of the vocal cords to come into close approximation. When the cords are not brought into proximity the breath flows out through the opened glottis unchecked and is wasted. Under such conditions it is utterly impossible to produce either a beautiful tone or have enough breath to sing phrases of even moderate difficulty with comfort.

The teacher who seeks to alleviate the breathless condition of the student, whose voice works poorly, by attempting to control the rate of expulsion is perpetrating the grossest injustice. Yet what alternative is there to offer? Totally without knowledge of the manner of dividing the registers, of rejoining them by an undetectable mutation after each has been developed separately, or of the urgency of purifying the vowel quality in conformity with Bel Canto procedure, what is the instructor to do? Why, of course, it's all in the breathing!

As the subject matter of breathing techniques requires but little study for reasonable familiarity, almost anyone can set himself up as a professor of singing with only this limited knowledge of the subject at his disposal. It is not to be wondered at that so few of the many thousands of students who undertake to master the art of singing manage to get anything out of their instruction. Rationing the breath expulsion is always exceedingly dangerous, and there is convincing proof on all sides to support the claim that throatiness is the natural result of a controlled expiration.

One of the more obvious reasons why control over the rate of the breath expulsion is impossible is because each sung tone, depending upon its pitch and degree of intensity, requires a specific amount of energy. This source of energy is supplied by the amount of air compressed into the diaphragm. The breath pressure, therefore, should not be regulated or controlled because of any necessity for saving it, but solely for the purpose of meeting the energy requirements demanded by the pitch and intensity. To 'control' the breath invariably means to attempt to save it. To try to save it is to withdraw the very support and energy the tone requires for maintaining its efficiency.

A complete exposure of the inherent fallacy of attempting to control the breath involves a more minute examination of the vocal apparatus.

The act of breathing consists of inhaling and exhaling quantities of air. Each of these acts is performed by the activity of muscular contractions. On exhaling, the expiratory muscles are brought into tension, while inhalation is performed by tensing the inspiratory muscles. Whichever of the two muscles is active, the other must remain passive.

When either the inspiratory or the expiratory muscles are brought into tension the glottis, or the space between the vocal cords, widens to permit the free passage of air to or from the lungs. At the moment of transferal of tension, however, the glottal space closes momentarily only to open again upon the completion of the transfer. This is a reflex action and is beyond the singer's voluntary control. No direct effort should ever be made to influence or control this action.

It may readily be seen, therefore, that tension on either the inspiratory or the expiratory muscles during the act of singing constitutes a serious impediment to the free and independent action of the vocal cords. The element of conflict continually present is in effect the desire of the vocalist to approximate the vocal cords to produce tone, while the tension of the expiratory muscles used to direct the pressure of the breath against the vocal cords prohibits them from approximating. Therefore, some means must be devised whereby it will be possible to circumvent the opening action of the glottis as it responds to the tensed expiratory muscles. This may only be done by holding the *inspiratory* tension in perfect balance with the *expiratory* tension throughout singing.

At first glance the practice of holding the tension on the inspiratory muscles, even during the act of inspiration, would produce the same result as holding the tension on the muscles of expiration, since either group in tension widens the glottal space. The difference, however, is in making sure that the tension is caught and held at the precise moment of transfer. This leaves the two opposing muscular contractions in equal balance and the glottis remains closed. As the natural tendency of the breathing apparatus during the release of breath is to bring the muscles of *expiration* into action, the sense of firm hold on the inspiratory muscles cancels that inclination and the perfect balance between them can be maintained. It is imperative that the diaphragm *does not move inward* as the voice progresses through successive musical phrases.

Once an even balance of tension has been set up between the inspiratory and the expiratory muscles the singer is no longer able to force, or, for that matter, to deliberately hold back the breath without first destroying the balance created, thereby shifting to an expiratory tension. Tension evenly balanced and maintained as in a correct manner of breathing leads to a precision of attack, i.e., the instantaneous sounding of a definite pitch, vowel and intensity, otherwise impossible. All noise, breathiness and other impurities are simultaneously eliminated.

Under an arrangement where the inspiratory and expiratory tension is held in even balance the tone production takes on a buoyant quality and, if the registration is well developed and working harmoniously, the 'purity of intonation' so admired by all lovers of Bel Canto will have been attained. Breathing techniques, however, must always be considered subordinate to registration and vowel purity; not *responsible* for those conditions, but merely a co-operative element.

With the vocal cords in a position of approximation because the registers are functioning correctly and co-ordinating effectively with the breathing, the vibrato action will occur spontaneously. Because the vocal cords are able to draw closely together without resistance, the 'bowing action,' or escape of the breath by a series of rapid puffs, regulates the reduction of pressure. As only a minute quantity of breath escapes during the vibrato cycle there need be no concern over the possibility of a too rapid rate of emission.

The effect of intercostal breathing is one in which the breathing apparatus is used as a container, variable in size and content, into which air is compressed. It is the degree of compression that creates the source of energy each tone or phrase requires to be evenly sustained. In reality very little of the breath taken in is used, so that on the completion of a phrase the singer should have a quantity of breath left over and to spare. This quantity of breath should be released *before each new inspiration* and the muscles allowed a brief moment of relaxation before recommencing the cycle. Much of the skill in singing is developing an exact and rhythmic sense of 'timing' of the breathing mechanism.

The chief advantage of diaphragmatic, or intercostal, breathing is that the vocal cords are free to vibrate without interfering with the glottal movement. Even more important, this procedure permits all of the expired breath to be converted into tone with the result that the voice is clearly and purely emitted without being marred by breathiness, or other rasping qualities. Never is it permissible to try to achieve this goal by regulating the rate of the breath expulsion. The vocal cords can only act as a valve on the escaping breath when they are in a position of approximation. The cords may only be approximated by the creation of an even balance of tension on *both* the muscles of inspiration as well as those of expiration.

The conscious operation of the breathing apparatus in the manner suggested does not require the formation of unnatural habits, nor does the operation differ from breathing as it is normally performed. The only essential difference between breathing in singing, as against that practiced during ordinary circumstances of living, is that singing demands a constant source of pressure which can only be supplied by a pair of well-filled lungs. Because it is a natural way of breathing, more often than not this technique is readily grasped and adopted instinctively as the fundamental principles of vocal technique are mastered. It is of great importance not to overestimate this comparatively trivial aspect of tone production and attribute curative powers to special techniques of breathing they do not possess. *172*

CHAPTER X

DECLINE OF BEL CANTO

The decades following upon the seventeenth and eighteenth centuries, at which time the Bel Canto style of singing was best understood and most frequently attained, were marked by a general preservation of the principles laid down by those who had established the tradition.

Many familiar names form a link connecting the present with the past, and those of Caccini, Tosi, Mancini, Casselli, Aprili, Bordogni, Roncini, the two Lampertis (father and son), Concone, the two Garcias (also father and son) and, finally, Matilde and Salvatore Marchesi who, together with their daughter Blanche, conspicuously endeavored to preserve the continuity.

Despite the efforts of these standard-bearers the art of Bel Canto singing, unfortunately, is now virtually extinct. Many have claimed that the disappearance of Bel Canto is the result of a practice, by those who had attained the greatest insight into the voice-building process, of withholding and secreting information as to proper procedures. This viewpoint, however, is untenable inasmuch as so many vocalists had mastered the art so thoroughly. The early teachers were not cultists, nor were their students sworn to secrecy. Many of the obstacles barring our understanding have been of our own making and will only be removed after we have become aware of the inaccuracy of most of our present opinions regarding voice.

The necessity is now urgent to review without bias the substance of these opinions. Once having done this, sound judgment will incline us to return to, and re-establish, those principles of tone production so clearly enunciated in the declarations of the early teachers of Bel Canto.

One of the primary purposes of this book has been to remove Bel Canto from its present position in the realm of esoteric mysteries and reintroduce it to the world of reality and common experience. With this purpose uppermost in mind an attempt will be made to prove that Bel Canto has not been lost as a realistic technique of tone production because of zealously guarded 'secrets,' but for very practical reasons.

The reasons for the inevitable decline of Bel Canto as a singing style are three in number: first, confusion growing out of nomenclature; second, the appearance of the 'virtuoso' teacher; and third, entry of the scientific investigator into the field of vocal endeavor.

The first breach in the armor of the old tradition was nomenclature. Many teachers now seem to be in agreement on certain fundamental issues and appear to talk a common and mutually intelligible language. Experience, however, has often shown that in reality the disparity between what has been said and what is actually understood to have been said or, for that matter, what was thought to have been said and what was actually said, is very wide indeed. Thus, the failure of the now numerous shades of theoretical opinion to reach agreement on fundamental issues is in a large measure the failure of language to supply a suitable and mutually understood vocabulary to adequately describe the mechanical action of the vocal organs.

Even the early masters were unable to circumvent the language barrier and were guilty of introducing terms susceptible of several interpretations. The investigator seeking to determine the causes contributing to the initial impairment of Bel Canto need only inquire into this phraseology to find one of the solutions to the mystery of its disappearance.

In the early days each register was known by two names. The lower was either called the *voce di piena*, meaning 'full voice,' or *voce di petto*, the 'voice of the chest.' The second register of sounds was equally familiar as the *falsetto*, or the *voce di testa*, the 'voice of the head.'

From this description of the registers it may be assumed that the early teachers considered tone production from two separate viewpoints: one recognizing that each group of sounds possessed innate qualities of contour and type, as 'full' and 'false,' the other acknowledging those sensations of vibration felt in the 'head' and 'chest' whenever resonant tones had been sung. This latter viewpoint was and is of exceedingly dubious value and ultimately proved to be the first adverse influence undermining the structure of Bel Canto, for when the primary emphasis on singing pure vowels within a rigid register definition was shifted to vague and ill-defined 'sensations of vibration' many interpretations of questionable expediency began to appear.

While realizing that resonant tones create the illusion of vibrations having been concentrated in either the 'head' or the 'chest,' it is not recorded that the early teachers ever stressed this phase of singing, and it has only been in comparatively recent years that any importance has been attached to such considerations. All earlier mention of the 'head' and 'chest' registers clearly stated that these terms were synonymous with the "falsetto' and the 'full' voice.

When excessive emphasis was finally drawn in later years to 'sensations of vibration' the instruction was at once removed to perilous ground. Instead of crediting a correct registration with being the direct cause of localized vibrations of the 'head' and 'chest,' the sensations of tone were made an end in themselves and were sought after as a means for establishing a correct mechanical response of the vocal mechanism.

The effect of having thus transferred the emphasis disclosed, with the passing of time, a serious distortion of the basic elements of Bel Canto instruction. Instead of being justly considered a specific type of sound which any student can readily produce by the simple process of imitation, the *voce di testa*, or voice of the head, came to indicate the area of resonance, therefore the logical target for 'projecting' the tone.

From the fallacy of tonal projection other ideas constituting a further departure from the original instruction arose. The student must learn to 'place his voice forward' and 'feel the tone in the head.' Likewise, the *voce di petto*, or voice of the chest, drew attention of many teachers to the sensations of tone accompanying the act of singing in the chest register. This led to another departure as concepts of 'high' and 'low' placement began to develop.

Judging from a standpoint of practical pedagogy, nothing was gained by de-emphasizing earlier concepts of a register as a sound quality and shifting the student's attention to vague and elusive sensations of vibration. Far from being practical, the supposition that a well-resonated tone is the inevitable result of having 'brought the tone forward' is totally unwarranted and contrary to the known and established principles of acoustics. The extent of this delusion is demonstrated by singers themselves, most of whom believe implicitly in the 'forwardness' of their production despite the fact so very few of them sing even passably well.

To attempt to learn to sing by trying to experience a sense of vibration in localized parts of the anatomy is both futile and dangerous. Two insuperable obstacles forever bar the realization of this objective as long as these means are employed: (1) because no matter how graphically the various symptoms of vibratory sensation may be described, they forever remain meaningless unless one has already experienced an identical feeling of vibration because of a naturally well-advanced condition of vocal technique, and (2) because the type of sensation experienced is the *result of the type of tone that has been produced and not its cause.*

All experienced singers are, of course, deeply sensitive to the proper 'feel' of the tones they produce. It is foolish, however, to depend upon this reaction to provide a sound basis for a technique of tone production. Groping for a new and more desirable sensation of resonance is much too elusive and intangible a procedure to be helpful to a student. On the other hand, it is easily possible to change the type of sensation experienced by readjusting the registration. Establishing the registers *di petto* and *di testa* quickly awakens vibrations in the 'chest' and in the 'head,' so that singing in a correctly balanced registration is responsible for, and causes, 'head resonance,' or 'forward emission' and 'chest resonance.' Registration, however, is determined by pitch and intensity, not by trying to experience localized vibrations.

The first departure from Bel Canto procedure, therefore, began when the channels of pedagogical thought were directed away from clear concepts of registration and vowel purity into the mystical realm of 'sensations of vibration.' After the 'head' voice had received wide acceptance as a suitable name for the falsetto there soon followed a centering of attention on other phases of vibratory sensations. Singing in the 'head' voice created the impression that the tone had been 'brought forward,' leading, in its turn, to the assumption that it had been 'placed.' The exact place, however, has long been a moot question and authorities today no longer agree either on the means of finding it, of its precise location or, indeed, whether there exists such a 'place' at all.

The culminating point of this type of instruction is found in the work of a singer who achieved distinction as one of the world's truly great artists, both vocally and musically. In her book *How to Sing*, Madame Lilli

Lehmann devotes endless pages to descriptions of the vocal sensations she experienced in singing, as though an attempt to duplicate them could possibly be successful.

The topics Madame Lehmann discusses under separate headings are 'Sensation and Position of the Tongue,' 'The Sensations of the Palate,' 'The Head Voice,' 'The Sensation of the Nose,' and 'The Sensation of the Resonance of the Head Cavities.' The following quotation will offer a fair sample of the labyrinthian paths into which the student is diverted by this approach. As so many of the statements made are so obviously the sheerest nonsense, no effort will be made to demonstrate the many fallacies.

'One of the most important positions closely connected with the first breath-jerk is provided by the dilation of the nostrils, the lifting and pushing of the backward nasal wall toward the so-broadened nose which in turn widens the pillars of the fauces and enables them to co-operate. The soft palate and the pillars of the fauces have a firm hold at the nose and a point of resistance upon which they can continually, according to necessity, heighten and lower themselves without having to change the position given them by this support.

'As soon as the nose is adjusted by the breath-jerk and with it the $\bar{a}$ is placed by the larynx, the $y\bar{e}$ position must be joined to the A, this brings the tone forward toward the nose and lets it ring over the lowered palate, as by means of the $y\bar{e}$ the tongue compels the larynx to take a higher backward position and thus constricts the cavity of the mouth. The sensation would appear thus: $-a-$ horizontally alone and $\bar{a}y\bar{e}$ joined to it. The y and the $\bar{e}$ are felt firmly at the nasal wall. The slanting $-a-$ which represents the frontal lowering of the larynx, pushes with its $\bar{a}$-strength toward the chest muscles in the front and so, always replaced and re-articulated, comes to be placed under the strongly tensed nasal wall where it must always remain.' (30).

There is not the slightest doubt but that all this detail which, incidentally, runs on through almost three hundred pages of her book had a very real meaning for Madame Lehmann. It can, and must, however, be questioned as a sound procedure for basic training. In the first place, Madame Lehmann never *learned* to sing by this method as her own voice was from earliest child hood quite phenomenal. She herself tells how, as little children, she and her sister Marie could strike the fourth line C a hundred times in succession and trill on it for a long time, and that they used to sing the aria of the Queen of the Night from Mozart's *The Magic Flute*, a feat few singers in history have been able to accomplish as adults. Madame Lehmann's vocal co-ordination, therefore, was natural rather than acquired and, of course, her entire sensitivity was bound together by the proper 'feel' of the mechanical adjustments involved.

The supreme difficulty in making this approach practical is that every singer experiences, according to the condition of his vocal technique, a wide variety of physical sensations, some of which can either be ignored or recognized as it suits one's own fancy. Thus, while Madame Lehmann was keenly sensitive to numerous sensations of the throat and head, others, less imaginative, have been content with simpler aids. Witherspoon felt the tone 'almost *in* the lower back of the nose,' Caruso frequently observed a 'tingling sensation in his legs,' Jean de Reszke felt all vibratory sensations in the 'masque,' while Italian singers in general usually imagine themselves to be directing the tone 'at the lips.'

Sensations of the kind described may appear full of meaning and of great help to the particular individual whose vocal technique, or imagination, awakens such experiences of vibration. To the average student, however, especially the beginner, this approach to voice training is hopelessly confusing and thoroughly unintelligible. Other developments growing out of attempts to describe and imitate sensations of resonance have led to such inaccurate and loose expressions as, 'feel that you grow bigger as the tone swells,' 'sing with a floating jaw,' 'keep the throat as in the act of drinking,' 'hold the throat as in yawning,' or 'feel the tone as an expanded and flexible tube, extending from the base of the lungs to the lips.'

Little justification exists for the continuance of instruction built on such a flimsy foundation, and the sooner it is abandoned for more substantial guides the more quickly satisfying will be the results. In short, all that has been accomplished by instruction devoted to descriptions of vibratory sensations is to remove all emphasis from the *causes* that give rise to these sensations and dwell on the *result* of a correct mechanical action instead.

The first error in thinking, therefore, occurred when the procedure of the early masters in developing mental pictures of sound patterns and tonal relationships was reversed by drawing the student's attention to sensations he either feels or ought to feel. An effect was made the cause of tone production and, with the lapse of time, the nature of the cause was completely lost. With the cause obscured the principles indispensable to correct tone production seemed either superfluous or incomprehensible, and the entire point of all earlier instruction rendered meaningless.

A further clouding over of the basic principles of tone production took place after a number of teachers became individually prominent as experts. It is only reciting history to relate that singers the world over flocked to the Lampertis, the Garcias, the Marchesis and others of comparable reputation. Those chosen for study often learned to sing better, and many became magnificent artists. But what they did not learn was the importance of returning to the prime fundamentals of vocal technique after they, in their turn, became teachers.

Few vocalists who are successful performers have either the time or the inclination to carry out a thorough investigation of the history and development of voice-training methods. In a life crowded with learning repertoire, making public appearances, and filling social obligations such independent studies generally have no place. Therefore, when the proper time arrived to take up the duties of teaching, those who had once been leading singers taught only those principles of tone production made known to them by *their* teachers, and the mistake consistently made has been in merely duplicating a pedagogic procedure they themselves had experienced as students. These procedures, unfortunately, were not generally applicable and, as such, had a decidedly limited value.

For this reason alone many brilliant vocalists, even apart from the fact that they are often temperamentally incompatible with the general discipline of a teacher's life, have been miserable failures in this branch of the art. Many have been taught to sing, but few have studied to be teachers. This is not enough, and an investigation of the circumstances surrounding their selection as protégés will reveal how this came about.

Unlike the instrumentalist who must systematically progress through a series of graded exercises to acquire manual dexterity and skill, the singer may have a perfect vocal technique without ever having had a lesson. Thus, there are instances where singers have become world famous without ever having studied voice. On the other hand, others have studied diligently for six or more years without having progressed beyond the first lesson.

As the voices selected for training by the virtuoso teacher were outstanding and mechanically, by a happy circumstance of nature, in excellent working order the absolute necessity for 'dividing the voice into two registers' and the procedure of 'unifying their action' became exigencies of lesser moment for the very good reason that a favorable condition and balance between the registers already existed. As the problem of registration, always most acute with the average beginner, is not of the most pressing need with those who are already technically proficient, all subsequent instruction began to shift from this basic fundamental to the niceties of the art. Smooth out the voice, polish the style, and the finished product emerges.

Great as they may have been as performers, what could singers trained under these conditions know of the mechanics of tone production? How could it be possible for them to help others when the only problems they had encountered were such relative trivialities as 'don't force,' 'sing pure vowels,' 'master a perfect legato,' 'keep the intensity scale even,' and 'breathing'? Anyone can operate a complicated piece of machinery when it is in good condition, but only a mechanic who fully understands the relationship and function of one part with the other is able to repair mechanical deficiencies and get the imperfectly functioning parts working smoothly and efficiently. Knowledge of the interrelationship and interdependency of the registers is tantamount to knowledge of the mechanics of tone production.

It need hardly be said that smoothing out the voice and polishing the style is not really voice 'building' at all, for the voice so richly endowed by nature has already been built. Marchesi, who claimed the celebrated Melba as her pupil, never 'built' that great voice, or provided it with the flawless technique for which the *prima donna* was so justly renowned, simply because the nine months of study Melba had with her prior to making a sensational debut was too short a time to do more than polish the technique. Because of the ideal conditions under which the 'virtuoso' teacher worked, therefore, many important fundamental principles of the art of singing became blurred and indistinct. As teachers of lesser artistic perception were incompetent to preserve these principles the second step toward the decline of Bel Canto had been made.

The full extent of the difference between the principles of Bel Canto laid down by the early masters, as compared with the practices of later and supposed exponents, is more clearly shown in the following table. Here the importance attached to the several aspects of tone production in three different periods of vocal history may be judged.

DECLINE OF BEL CANTO

17th & 18th CENTURY PROCEDURES*
of Caccini Tosi and Mancini

1. Sight singing
2. Vowel formation
3. Establish chest and falsetto registers in all voice types
4. Develop each register as a separate entity
5. Blend registers by perfect mutation
6. Simultaneous development of following in order of difficulty:
    - (a) Solfeggi
    - (b) Legato
    - (c) Portamento
    - (d) Easy embellishments
    - (e) Difficult embellishments
    - (f) Messa di voce
    - (g) Agility
7. Emphasis on pure vowel quality throughout

* All exercises were performed a cappella

19th CENTURY PROCEDURES*
of Lamperti and Garcia

1. Breathing
2. Resonance
3. Vowel formation
4. Sostenuto
5. Legato
6. Portamento
7. Messa di voce
8. Agility
9. Subject of registers touched upon lightly and essentially in agreement with earlier procedures

-Gradual transition to accompanied exercises

LATE 19th & 20th CENTURY PROCEDURES
of Shakespeare, Schoen-René and other moderns

1. Breathing
2. Relaxation
3. Agility
4. Voice 'placing'
5. Support of tone
6. Singing on the breath
7. Open throat

The only noteworthy difference between the techniques of Bel Canto employed by Tosi and Mancini, as compared with the work of Lamperti and Garcia (and the second listing is Garcia's own), is demonstrated, when examined, to be in a reversal of the importance of registration and breathing. The third classification showing the opinions entertained by modern and supposed exponents of Bel Canto demonstrates nothing, of course, except the complete absence of any similarity between present-day methods and earlier practices. The entire outline of Tosi's and Mancini's procedure is made up of factual and concrete principles any student can readily follow and perform, while the modern proposals are full of empty and meaningless terms impossible of execution and devoid of significance.

Although the published works of Garcia and the elder Lamperti freely discuss the problems of registration, and include a table of staffs showing the outlines and boundaries marking the position of each, nevertheless their enthusiasm for this phase of tone production remained somewhat casual. Because of their immense reputations they were obliged to accept as pupils only those who were exceedingly gifted and whose advanced technical status made the problem of registration and register development a matter of secondary concern. However, by discussing the position and importance of the registers *di petto* and *di testa* in both male and female voices they clearly indicated their acceptance of these two parts as a natural function and importantly related to a sound vocal technique. What they failed to show adequately is the absolute necessity for establishing each of the registers at the inception of training, especially with poorly used voices, which for that very reason are not cleanly divided into two parts. Also, their failure to clarify the position of the 'middle' register in the three divisions they acknowledged to exist contributed largely to what now amounts to a general misunderstanding of the entire subject of registration. As a result of this misunderstanding, only those who are gifted by nature with a voice that is already well produced are now able to entertain the hope of achieving a place in the profession, whereas in former years it was not the amount of voice one started with that was so important as innate musicianship and talent for singing. Correct application of the fundamental principles of Bel Canto alone can 'build' a voice and provide the world with singers who are both well-schooled vocalists and fine musicians.

The more superficial principles of Bel Canto supported by Garcia and Lamperti soon gained acceptance as representing the prime fundamentals of vocal technique. Yet, even though almost all of the really profoundly constructive properties of the earlier instruction had been removed, nevertheless many eminently useful precepts indispensable to good singing remained intact. If talented pupils with faulty tone production could not be appreciably helped or improved by these latter methods, naturally fine voices were not only improved, but preserved. More serious elements of deterioration began to manifest themselves when peculiar terminology such as 'forward placement,' 'nasal resonance,' 'breath control,' and concepts of singing as 'vocalized breath' gained universal acceptance and came to be looked upon as the legitimate causes of beautiful tone production.

Garcia the younger was a unique figure in the history of music. After a brief career as a singer and impresario he entered the teaching profession in which capacity he labored for seventy-five years. Without doubt he faithfully helped to perpetuate during his earliest years as a teacher those principles of Bel Canto he had learned from his father and other predecessors. No evidence has ever been submitted to indicate that he had ever at any time disagreed with the theories and principles of Bel Canto he had learned as a young student. His only cause for dissatisfaction with the old system was the length of time necessary to obtain vocal mastery.

In order to find a short cut to vocal mastery Garcia conducted numerous experiments with the purpose of gaining a direct control over the vocal organs themselves uppermost in mind. Thus, it was he who in a lifetime of teaching introduced many theories widely at variance with the practices of the early masters. Many of the ideas of tone production initiated by him are still in vogue today, and the complete disappearance of the old system of training is to a very great extent his responsibility. These errors of commission he partially rectified in a retraction published in the London *Musical Herald*, August 1894. In this statement Garcia refutes many of the principles he once supported and which, despite his refutation, have through association with his name since gained an almost world-wide acceptance. This is his advice:

'Avoid all these modern theories and stick closely to Nature. I do not believe in teaching by means of sensations of tone. The actual things to do in producing tone is to breathe, to use the vocal cords, and to form the tone in the mouth. The singer has to do with nothing else. I began with other things; I used to direct the tone in the head, and do peculiar things with the breathing, and so on, but as the years passed by I discarded them as useless, and now speak only of actual things and not mere appearances. I condemn that which is spoken of nowadays, viz., the directing of the voice forward, or back and up. Vibrations come from puffs of air. All control of the breath is lost the moment it is turned into vibrations, and the idea is absurd that a current of air can be thrown against the hard palate for one kind of tone, the soft palate for another, and reflected hither and thither. With regard to the position of the larynx, higher or lower, the singer need only follow natural emotional effects, and larynx, palate and the rest will take care of themselves. As to breathing, do not complicate it with theories, but take an inspiration and notice Nature's laws.'

The statement of Garcia quoted above is of exceptional interest and value. Not only does it betray the many-sided interests of an alert and inquiring mind, but it shows that after a lifetime of teaching the experience he had gained compelled him to return to the abandoned procedures he had originally inherited from his father and other predecessors. He himself had authored many of the newer developments in voice-training methods yet after seventy years of practical experience his counsel is to 'avoid all these modern theories' and 'stick closely to Nature.' Full well he came to realize the importance of the psychological factors involved in training the voice, and that the physical response of the vocal mechanism can only be brought under the singer's control by developing a high sensitivity to the value of tonal relationships. To 'observe Nature's laws' is merely to become aware of the vocal reaction to the instruction given. If the devices used cause the voice to increase in power, width of range, flexibility and ease of execution, then Nature's laws have been obeyed.

In judging the extent of one's agreement with Nature's laws, the example of the early teachers of Bel Canto provides a pattern by which progress can be measured. The estimated time for them to produce a fine voice is known to have been six years. Within this time it should be possible to bring the voice to its fullest maturity and mechanical perfection. At the end of this period of training, the voice should be able to sing loudly and softly, swell and diminish, possess a variety of 'color,' and have a range extending from a minimum of two and one-half to three octaves. Failure to achieve this goal may be attributed to either one, or both, of two factors. One, lack of talent and ability to work on the part of the student, and two, because the principles of vocal technique employed by the teacher are applied without understanding or insight, or otherwise do not conform to Nature's laws.

As a teacher Garcia for many years followed the traditional precepts of Bel Canto as he had learned them from his father and early associates. With the dawn of the scientific era and general speedup of everyday life by mechanization and industrialism, however, he grew somewhat restive and impatient with the slow-but-sure procedures of voice training and sought some means of shortening the period of apprenticeship heretofore understood to be indispensable to vocal mastery. With this object in mind he invented the laryngoscope, by means of which it became possible to observe the operation of the vocal cords and study their variable response to pitch, vowel and intensity.

The laryngoscope is a very simple instrument consisting of two mirrors. One, which must be very small, is attached to the end of a long metal shaft. This shaft may be inserted into the singer's mouth, with the mirror placed in such a way as to have the reflecting surface directed toward the vocal cords. While the smaller mirror is being held suspended at, but not against, the ceiling of the post-nasal pharynx, the larger mirror is placed so as to throw light rays upon it. Caught in this way, the movements of the vocal cords are reflected and it becomes possible for the operator of the device to study their action.

Several weaknesses seriously detract from the value of the laryngoscope. One is the difficulty of singing normally while suffering the inconvenience of having the mirror touch the uvula, or even suspended in the mouth cavity. Another obstacle is the limited visibility due to the obstruction of the tongue, as only a portion of the vocal cords are visible even with the aid of the mirrors. Garcia himself confessed having been denied the opportunity of viewing more than two thirds of the cords, as the anterior portion of the glottis was always concealed by the epiglottis.

To peer at the vocal cords through mirrors could hardly be called 'scientific investigation,' yet this procedure was the first step in that direction. Probably the first effort to discover the inner working of the vocal mechanism was made by the French physician Ferrein who published a treatise on the vocal organs as early as 1741. Voice teachers showed no interest in the physiological aspects of tone production at that time, however, and curiosity as to the probable construction of the vocal organs was completely ignored, as far as the vocal profession was concerned, up to the time of Garcia.

Shortly after Garcia made public the results of his laryngoscopic discoveries a veritable flood of earnest investigators became actively engaged in similar research and a new era in voice training had begun. The first to invade the field were medical doctors, or those possessing some knowledge of anatomy, and soon publications began to appear that were strongly reminiscent of the era of quack medicinal remedies. Abashed by their own ignorance of scientific matters the traditionalists remained silent in the face of what they considered irrefutable opinions and deferred to a power they felt unqualified and ill-equipped to combat.

In reality, however, there was very little to fear and only a short time elapsed before the scientific investigators themselves were working at cross purposes and with an astonishing absence of agreement. Sir Morell Mackenzie very ably described the situation as it existed during the latter part of the nineteenth century, and as continues to exist today, when he stated, 'The immediate effect of the laryngoscope was to throw the whole subject into almost hopeless confusion by the introduction of all sorts of errors of observation, each claiming to be founded on ocular proof and believed in with corresponding obstinacy.'

The situation described by Mackenzie is informative and generally accurate except for one statement. What he described as 'all sorts of errors of observation' need not necessarily be so considered. Each observer had probably proceeded carefully and the conclusions drawn were doubtless formed with reasonable accuracy, but the reason for the wide disparity in their findings was unavoidable because of the technical condition of the voices available for study. Most observers were, like Garcia, men with a smattering of scientific knowledge, but primarily voice teachers collaborating with doctors and anatomists. In all probability their conclusions were based on observations made on their own students. As their pupils must have acquired a type of technique peculiar to the instruction they had received, it is more than likely the particular pattern of the vocal cord segmentation would also correspond, as the pattern of one teacher's pupils would quite obviously not agree with the pattern of those who had received a different type of voice training.

Madame Seiler was one of the first to become aware of this possibility and protested vehemently when the published results of her laryngoscopic discoveries were criticized and disputed by rival 'authorities.' It was her contention that those changes of adjustment for the first and second chest and falsetto mechanisms she believed to exist, would only be observed in persons who had been properly trained, or in those whose vocal technique was in a 'natural' condition and not impaired by faulty teaching procedures. It was her position that the question was being unfairly treated when those who had been subjected to systems of teaching at variance with her methods were submitted to examination and then used as examples to disprove the theories she supported.

This contention, of course, strikes at the very root of the problem of all investigations of this kind. Analyzing the vocal cord action is without benefit for two compelling reasons. The first is that the correct action is not necessarily being performed. The second is that even if a number of perfect singers were available and sufficient factual data obtained to substantiate and establish the correct position and segmentation of the cords for each pitch, vowel and intensity, the inability of the student to duplicate the arrangement by a volitional act renders the knowledge worthless. As for the teacher, it is only necessary for the qualified instructor to *hear* the voice to know what is wrong with it. *Looking* at the vocal organs in action contributes nothing that is useful.

The fact is self-evident that no satisfactory use can be made of any knowledge derived from studying the vocal cord action as long as the performer is unable to directly control the manner in which the cords vibrate and segment. Imagine a voice lesson where the teacher looks through the laryngoscope and then after duly considering the situation solemnly informs his student, 'Your vocal cords are vibrating along their full length which is an incorrect position for the pitch you are singing. Only permit them to vibrate at their outer edges for the higher tones and shorten the length of the vibrating surface. Then you will find your production will be freer and easier. This way you will learn to produce more beautiful tones.' Try it!

The next step in the evolutionary process of scientific investigation was the promulgation of theories of tone production based upon the observations made through the laryngoscope. What each investigator saw he expanded into a theory. As every observer saw something different there were soon almost as many theories as there were investigators.

The fanatical zeal with which students, later becoming teachers, support the theories advanced by their own instructors is indeed unfortunate. Regardless of whether they had successfully mastered a sound technique of tone production, indeed, in spite of the fact that many of them had their careers cut short prematurely because of unsound training, these disciples remain faithful to what they had 'learned' and are ever ready to perpetuate even the most extraordinary nonsense. Few seem to think of measuring the actual accomplishments of these theories, or otherwise to test them to discover whether they merit such unbounded enthusiasm.

From the minor differences in the nomenclature of the early masters, who were otherwise in almost total agreement, vocal terminology became increasingly obscure. A condition is now prevalent where it is almost impossible for two students or two vocal teachers to discuss matters bearing on vocal technique without being almost completely in the dark about what the other is trying to say or, should their language be intelligible, without having the substance of their discourse provoke a direct antagonism.

Before entering further into a discussion of the development of scientific training methods it would be helpful, by way of contrast, to show the empirical nature of Bel Canto procedure as well as the significance of empiricism itself.

Empiricism is knowledge growing out of experience. The validity of empiricism, however, is often questionable because the knowledge fails to penetrate beyond mere appearances. Certain things *seem* to be so because under prescribed conditions they always work out the same. Nothing is proved, and no *fact* as it is known and recognized by the scientific world is established inasmuch as the causes remain unknown.

The weakness of empiricism as a basis for arriving at decisions and judgments is best illustrated by the relationship in the solar system between the sun and the earth. On the basis of visual evidence one is led to conclude that the sun revolves around the earth, when the *fact* is quite the opposite. Thus, where science deals with known quantities and proceeds from the known into the unknown, empiricism is a conclusion based upon experience and observation, therefore subject to error.

The virtue of empiricism with regard to its adaptability to voice training is that while the principles may be proven without factual basis and be 'unscientific,' the association of these principles with the conditions under which they were found adaptable proved favorable to correct tone production. *In fine*, the system worked! If only the scientific investigators could have explained *why* these principles worked satisfactorily, the teaching profession would have been helped immeasurably. Everyone knows that there is no 'voice of the chest,' or 'voice of the head,' if these expressions are taken literally, but there is no doubt that these terms denoting a register were full of meaning when properly understood.

Far from offering constructive analysis, however, the investigators proceeded to tear down every vestige of the traditional approach and substituted new theories, unproved and utterly without practical value. Unproved, because never in the entire history of singing has the laboratory technician and vocal scientist who taught on the principles he himself, or his confrères, championed, come forward and said, 'Here is the product of our research: here is the great singer, the perfect vocal technician only a scientific, fool-proof method can produce.'

Although they may be said to be dealing with 'facts,' nevertheless the work of the vocal scientist can hardly be said to be 'scientific' at all. If the results alone are judged it is apparent that the supposed factual data is either incomplete, in disarray, inappropriate to the situation in which it is being used, or not factual at all.

The position of the vocal scientist toward voice building has been clearly stated by Stanley in *The Science of Voice*, published as early as 1929. In a challenging announcement holding high hope for the future of singing he proclaimed, 'actually it is absolutely possible for the competent teacher to "make a voice" by application of the laws of vocal technique which are based on well-understood laws of physics and physiology.' (51). He then goes on to say, 'our knowledge of the laws governing the technic of singing has also advanced and it is possible to accomplish today what was utterly impossible for, say, the teacher of the old Italian school of Bel Canto.' Perfect!

With the knowledge of the laws of physics and physiology at the command of the scientific voice teacher it is logical to assume, therefore, that all misconceptions heretofore experienced in voice training should have become a thing of the past. So the present, with a number of teachers supposedly possessing a scientific skill and knowledge beyond anything that has been known before, should be the most brilliant 'Golden Age of Song' known to musical history! Obviously there is no 'Golden Age of Song' at the present time, *nor have singers trained in the science laboratory been found qualified to appear successfully on the opera or concert stage in sufficient numbers, if at all, to credit their development to scientific methods.*

It remains a source of considerable wonder to note the incredible facility most 'scientific' voice teachers have for overlooking the accomplishments of teachers of earlier generations and failing to profit by their experience. Surely there must be something to learn from the statements of the elder Lamperti and other early masters. Lamperti alone in his lifetime trained over forty singers who performed throughout the great opera houses of Europe as front rank artists. A few of them, Albani, Campanini, La Grange, Cruvelli, etc., were numbered among the greatest singers of any age. Is it possible that this could have been through sheer chance or accident?

An interesting insight is provided into the thinking of the vocal scientist when a statement appearing in a trade magazine by a Chicagoan discussing the teaching of Porpora, Mengozzi and Bernacchi writes of 'the chief reason for their pedagogic confusion.' Pedagogic confusion, indeed!

The late Oscar Thompson correctly labeled the results of so-called 'scientific' methods of voice production and theory when he wrote in the *International Cyclopedia of Music and Musicians*, 'the exceptions presented by various reputable dissenters are sufficiently strong to leave the "vocal science" of today in a most unscientific position.'

Before briefly outlining the essential features of vocal science as it is now known and practiced, it might be advantageous to show the purpose of the new trend. Primarily, the purpose of scientific voice training is to determine and establish basic principles of tone production and to provide a formula which will serve to shorten the length of time heretofore deemed necessary to master a correct technique of singing, as well as reduce the possibility of error in training procedures to a minimum. These aims are irreproachable but have long been championed by many teachers, past and present, whose knowledge of science is exceedingly limited. The main point of departure between the old and the new is in transferring the emphasis from a psychological approach to one almost exclusively concerned with physiology and acoustics.

To apply the latest developments of modern science toward facilitating vocal study is most desirable and a trend to be encouraged. However, up to the present time nothing has been accomplished toward clarifying the already confused state of voice-training methods because so far the vocal scientists are merely groping to discover basic principles. The handicap presently imposed on the sincere teacher of voice is the theorizing advanced by a few 'authorities,' some of whom are ex-singers posing as scientists, others, scientists posing as teachers of voice.

To be accurate, there is no such thing in existence at the present time as a 'science' of voice. Perhaps a start has been made in that direction, but at the moment there is no scientific method that will, when applied to the problems of training and developing the voice, either facilitate or perfect that training. If such a thing as a scientific method of voice training did exist, all talented students brought under the influence of such a training method should be quickly developed into superlative singers. Yet, the opposite is true, and the present decline in the art of singing has exactly corresponded to the rise of what should be more accurately termed 'pseudo scientific' methods. It should be of more than casual interest to the student of singing, therefore, to know something of the development of scientific methods as applied to vocal instruction.

A scientific method of singing was first sought after by Garcia and Helmholtz, each worker approaching the problem from a different starting point. Garcia chose to investigate the anatomical aspects of the subject, while Helmholtz directed his energies to fathoming the acoustical problems involved.

The methods of those who followed Garcia and sought to solve the mystery of the vocal action by studying the anatomical structure of the vocal organs are relatively straightforward and simple. As a beginning, the reaction of the vocal cords to pitch, vowel, intensity and registration were closely observed through the laryngoscope. Then most theorists began to compare the voice to some musical instrument such as the oboe, flute, violin, or clarinet. In this way a parallel was sought to help account for the ability of the vocal organs to produce beautiful, resonant tones over a wide pitch range.

Although the acoustical principles governing the response of the instruments used as comparisons with the voice are widely dissimilar in many important respects few analysts seemed to be disturbed by the contradictions. Before many fundamental issues had been solved, 'scientific' theories of tone production began to appear. The impression received after reading a quantity of the material published at that time is that greater effort was put forth to prove a theory than to ascertain a fact.

A typical example of the work of the vocal scientist as an anatomist may be gleaned from this excerpt on the subject by Charles Lunn, *The Philosophy of Voice*, who says, 'As the larynx ascends in the pipe, the speed of the ascent of the front part of the cricoid is swifter than that of the thyroid, so that the part of the cricoid in its upward progress gains on the ascent of its auxiliary, the thyroid. Hence, the vocal cords are tightened and the pitch of the voice is raised. In this ascent the thyroid and cricoid rotate on an eccentric centre, causing the planes of both the false and the true vocal cords to become with each heightened tone more slanting; thus, the sound, traveling at a right angle to these planes, finds its point of impact on the arch of the palate and more forward with each ascending sound.' (31). Just how this information is supposed to be helpful to the teacher or student of singing is not made clear. Mr. Lunn's reasoning, of course, was less influenced by facts than by a desire to prove to himself, as well as others, that the doctrine of 'forward placement' is supported by, and in agreement with, scientific laws. Few anatomists or acousticians, however, would risk their reputations by endorsing Mr. Lunn's claims.

Many, many volumes of similar pretention are to be found in libraries and bookstores. Essentially, all of these works are studies of anatomical and acoustical phenomena and are minutely descriptive and analytical. Usually each author announces that his method alone is 'scientific,' but few seem to offer concrete evidence to prove their contentions. Analytically many of these volumes are convincing, especially to those who have not been trained in the sciences, and therefore qualified to detect the errors of logic. Creatively, however, they all fall far short of the goal and standard set by the early masters of Bel Canto.

Success in training the voice is not dependent upon knowledge of muscles and muscular function. Neither does it follow that he who possesses insight into the anatomy of the vocal organs is able to control their action. A large majority of the greatest singers and teachers of singing in the entire history of music have never had the slightest scientific knowledge of anatomy, physics, or physiology. Conversely, great scientists have never been known to have been great singers, nor have scientists ever been noted as the trainers of outstanding singers.

The continued failure of the vocal scientist to teach others to sing or, in almost every case, to have ever sung themselves is only the logical outcome of the procedures they have chosen to adopt. To analyze the voice and show what is wrong with it is one thing. To rectify the condition is quite another! Analysis is very definitely the province of physics and acoustics, but to change the conditions as they have been found to exist is to enter the field of psychology. This must be so because neither the teacher nor the singer is able to control by direct and willful volition any of the *important* factors contributing to the harmonic content of the tone, i.e., quality. This can only be done by working *indirectly* through the registers and by applying the cardinal rule of maintaining a pure vowel quality.

Immediately the work of voice building is brought into the field of psychology, training procedures become a matter of learning to associate every tone quality produced with its probable physiological cause. The beautiful tone must be the perfectly produced tone and may be assumed to possess the requisite amount of overtone content in proportion to the fundamental, as well as other physical properties known to be desirable. Because the perfectly produced tone finds the mechanism working efficiently, powerful, resonant tones are produced with ease and freedom over a wide pitch range. Once having become familiar with the relationship of registration to intensity, and vowel quality to pure tone quality, tonal relationships and correct voice emission becomes a straightforward, uncomplicated, logical process easy to follow.

As the story of scientific investigation into matters of tone production unfolds, the realization of the futility of the physiological approach as a practical basis for developing the voice becomes more forcefully apparent. This will be shown both in the conflicting nature of the conclusions, and by demonstrating that the material findings surviving close scrutiny are always of such a kind as to preclude any hope of achievement by willful volition. The caliber of contemporary singing will improve just as soon as it is realized that deliberate regulation of 'the amount of the fleshy mass of the vocal cords exposed to the expiratory blast,' and debates as to whether or not the 'thyroid and the cricoid rotate on an eccentric centre' are relegated to purely academic discussions.

D. A. Clippinger in his book *The Head Voice and Other Problems* offered advice well taken by those who incline toward the scientific approach when he suggested, 'Stop looking at the voice and begin to listen to it.' (7).

The wisdom of Clippinger's statement is perhaps not fully realized by those who have not familiarized themselves with the development of scientific voice training. It hardly seems possible to believe anyone would actually stop listening to the voice in judging it. Yet, John Howard claims that the 'right way and the wrong way of singing is made appreciable by either *sight* or *touch*, or both.' Of course, vocal strain is clearly visible for all to see, but what an incredible idea it is to judge singing purely on that basis! Evidently it never occurred to Howard, and many other vocal scientists as well, that the right and the wrong way of singing can be *heard*.

With an ever-increasing number of investigators entering the field a wider diversity of opinion was continually being expressed as to the cause of a correct singing technique.

One of the first to display interest in physiological problems of voice, Sir Morell Mackenzie agreed with the early Italian theory of registration and considered the voice to be made up of two distinct parts. These he called the long reed' and the 'short reed,' because of the noticeable difference in the vocal cord segmentation for each mechanism. These fundamental alignments he likened to the *voce di petto* and the *voce di testa* of earlier usage.

The only difference between the voices of the two sexes Mackenzie believed to be expressed in the range of the voice. This is very much in accordance with earlier theoretical opinion. Mackenzie held that no voice differed from another mechanically but, as the female vocal organs are always smaller in size than those of the male, women sing an octave higher. Thus, the only difference in voice types is to be found in the size of the vocal organs and individual temperament. An exact parallel to this relationship may be found in the family of stringed instruments, where the violin, viola, violoncello and doublebass all operate on an identical mechanical principle. As with the voice, the discrepancies in size between the various members of the violin family cause a general shifting of the range, which in turn necessitates superficial differences and readjustments of technique.

John Howard, who might well be called the 'complete anatomist' because of his minute diagnosis of the physical reactions of the vocal mechanism, corroborates Mackenzie's conclusions and proves that the muscular arrangement of the vocal organs is so contrived as to allow only two registers. Emil Behnke, another prominent investigator during the late nineteenth century, however, disagreed with both Howard and Mackenzie and considered every voice to have three registers. These he referred to as 'thick,' 'thin' and 'small.' To make confusion worse confounded, Behnke capriciously subdivided these three groupings into 'lower thick and lower thin,' 'upper thick and upper thin,' and 'small.'

Madame Seiler, a distinguished pupil of Helmholtz, partially supports Behnke's opinion, but employs different terminology in her descriptions. She speaks of the registers as 'first and second chest,' and 'first and second falsetto,' with all tones lying above these four groups being the 'head' voice. Should any dissatisfaction be felt with these conclusions Dr. Reimann and Anatole Pilton offer other alternatives and state, 'we recognize four registers, the chest, head, middle and sombre.'

A greater majority of the observers, however, support the findings of Garcia who contended that only three mechanisms exist, the chest, middle and the head. Dr. Hunt, Charles Lunn, Lamperti, the three Marchesis, together with a host of others advocate this position, and this group has been so influential as to have succeeded in establishing the three-register theory to the point of its being an almost universally recognized fact.

Here and there a dissident element still maintains a direct opposition to all of the above theories of registration and declares the entire subject to be an illusion, or the product of bad singing. Led by Lilli Lehmann, Thorp and

Nicholl, those who support this contention recognize the voice as having but one register.

Few who have seriously studied the workings of the vocal organs subscribe to the single-register theory, however, and supporters of this claim are largely drawn from the ranks of singers who have by a coincidence of nature had the registers of their own voices indistinguishably joined. Personal vanity rather than reason has probably disposed these people to look with disfavor upon any other arrangement as being contrary to a correct or natural tone production. Lilli Lehmann, who denied the presence of registers in a properly produced voice, herself had a clearly defined register 'break' which has been preserved for all to hear in the recordings she made for posterity. Muzio, Boninsegna and many other famous singers also had a register 'break.' It is altogether improbable, however, that most of the greatest voices in history have had a divided registration because of an unnatural technique of tone production.

Some idea of the confusion which, like Topsy, 'just growed,' is indicated in the conflict of authoritative opinion developed since the invention of the laryngoscope. Those who advanced theories based upon visual evidence of the workings of the vocal cords alone have proven nothing except that there is general disagreement. Anatomists, on the other hand, who have traced with painstaking care the possible muscular functions conceivably involved have rarely found reason to believe more than two mechanisms could be operative. Thus, it is possible to find support from reasonably authentic sources of the earlier theory of registration as it was understood, although recognized purely as a sound phenomenon, by the early masters of Bel Canto.

The work of Dr. Holbrook Curtis is noteworthy in this regard, because he sums up and supports in a volume largely given over to a minute analysis of the anatomical, structure of the vocal organs and the muscular contractions influencing its function, many conclusions arrived at many, many years earlier by the teachers of Bel Canto. He declared:

'We *assume* that there are three registers, chest, medium and head, which need be considered in training the human voice; but we *believe* that there are but two distinct mechanisms and even the transition from one register to the other in singing the scale may be made practically imperceptible, if the proper method is employed.' (8).

This, of course, is the procedure practiced in Italy long before anatomy and physics entered the field of voice training.

All of the foregoing theories have evolved out of investigations conducted with the aid of the laryngoscope, or by studying the vocal response as an anatomical function. But these differences of opinion are not the only ones encountered. With regard to the falsetto, numerous contradictory beliefs further obscure the issue.

It was Garcia's opinion that the male falsetto was a remnant of the boy's voice. Some confusion has been caused by his statement because a superficial reading often conveys the impression that the falsetto was to be discarded as an unimportant part of the voice. Many have neglected to note the stress he placed on the falsetto being weak and effeminate *only because it is usually found undeveloped and in a state of general deterioration through disuse*. Garcia was specific in saying he considered the falsetto a legitimate part of the voice, especially with tenors who are incapable of producing their upper voice range effectively without it. In this respect his work again represents a departure from the experience of the earlier teachers of Bel Canto. It was their contention that the falsetto was important to *every* voice.

Attempts to explain the falsetto find the leading authorities in even greater conflict of opinion. Many accept Garcia's theory that the characteristic sound of this register is due to a peculiar segmentation of the vocal cords, but there are also a great many dissenters.

In this latter category Charles Lunn advances a theory purporting to prove that the action of the true vocal cords is not in any way involved in producing a falsetto tone. The peculiar quality of this register he attributes to a function of the false vocal cords. In this he is supported by Mantels who likewise insisted that the falsetto does not engage the action of the vocal cords to produce pitch. In his opinion the mechanism of the falsetto is similar to that of the flute. The flute, of course, has no vibrator. Instead, the pitch of the various tones comprising its compass is determined by regulating the length of the tube, or resonance chamber. When a quantity of air, blown by the player, passes in and out of the instrument the air contained within the walls of the flute pulsates according to the natural frequency of the tube. Thus, the necessity for having a vibrator is dispensed with.

Observation of the vocal cord action thoroughly dispels any serious consideration of the voice being a flute-like mechanism. If the laryngoscope proves nothing else, it shows that the true vocal cords do participate actively in falsetto. Other theories concerning the falsetto contend that this register owes its peculiar quality to the fact that the cords 'vibrate only on their outer rim,' or is 'dependent upon the position of the larynx,' 'arises from nodes,' or is the result of the vocal cords being 'insufficiently approximated.'

The most fantastic of all the opinions advanced to explain the falsetto is the belief of Dr. Alexander Guilmette (*Vocal Physiology*, 1878) who is of the opinion that neither the true nor the false vocal cords have anything whatever to do with the production of vocal tone. He ascribes the tones produced by the human voice to a function of the mucous membrane lining the trachea, larynx, pharynx and mouth.

Ernest G. White, in *Sinus Tone Production*, supports Dr. Guilmette's opinion, but with reservations, for he attributes the ability of the voice to produce pitch and resonate tones to the presence of the sinus cavities. White states unequivocally that the voice is a flute-like mechanism. Other authorities disagree and compare it to a reed instrument such as the oboe or clarinet. Professor Hallock and Dr. Muckey find no acoustic similarity between the voice and any of these instruments and present a counterclaim to the effect that the vocal cord action bears closer resemblance to a stringed instrument such as the violin.

In contradicting White's testimony on the importance of the sinus cavities Hallock and Muckey state, 'It is sometimes urged that these cavities, together with the antra, aid in resonance, but it is practically impossible, since at best their openings are small, and they are usually closed entirely, as is the cavity of the inner ear. A closed cavity cannot reinforce a tone.' (18).

The effect of the presence or absence of a correct vocal cord action on the quality of sound produced is another of the moot points long debated by the vocal scientists. Dr. Mills is emphatic in declaring that 'the vocal bands have little or nothing to do with the quality of the tone.' In this opinion Dr. Mills is supported by Helmholtz, whose experiments with the clarinet and other instruments demonstrated that the actual sound produced by the vibrating reed is not only infinitesimal in volume, but utterly lacking in quality and distinction.

John Howard and Helmholtz are most prominent among those who concur with Dr. Mills' conclusions and believe that tone quality is determined solely by the way in which the chambers of resonance are shaped.

In opposition to the findings of Dr. Mills are investigators of such eminence as Professor Scripture, Professor Hallock and Dr. Muckey. In concurring with Professor Scripture, Hallock and Muckey offer most compelling evidence in support of the importance of the vocal cord action when they say, 'It must be borne in mind that these overtones, whose vibrations enable us to articulate, and to put feeling in the voice, originate in the vocal cords themselves, and that they are modified only as to their relative intensity by the resonance cavities above.' Professor Scripture lends support to this argument by stating, 'the glottal lips vibrate differently for the different vowels.'

In recent years there has come into vogue a belief in the doctrine of 'nasal resonance.' The first enthusiasts for this method of tone production were Dr. Holbrook Curtis and the tenor Jean de Reszke. Between them they share the responsibility for establishing and then, despite having witnessed its obvious failure, helping to perpetuate one of the most ugly and destructive forms of voice production imaginable. An example of the futility of nasal resonance as a basis for correct tone production has long been, and is continually being, demonstrated by French singers, or those who employ the French style, whose 'white,' 'thin,' 'pinched,' non-resonant, inexpressive, off-pitch singing has long been the rule rather than the exception. Only in the rarest instances does a singer trained in the French style acquire a technique which keeps the voice fresh and youthful after many years of arduous singing. Contrary to belief, the problem of the French nasals can be reconciled with the principles of Bel Canto.

The position of Dr. Curtis in the musical world was that of a laryngologist who for many years had specialized in relieving singers of throat troubles brought on by incorrect or overextended singing. Toward the close of his singing career Jean de Reszke was one of his patients. Between them they ultimately arrived at the conclusion that the vocal cords were too weak and fragile to withstand the rigors of operatic singing. In order to relieve the cords of all pressure built up by tension De Reszke and Curtis struck upon the idea of letting the head cavities assume the burden of effort.

Although the thought was not framed in so many words it is probable that their intent was similar in kind to White's; namely, to subordinate the vocal cords and employ the voice as an acoustic device identical with the flute, which requires no vibrator.

If the results of his work had not been such a tragic blow to the art of singing, in many respects Dr. Curtis's book is amusing. In his analysis of the muscular operation of the vocal mechanism Dr. Curtis finds it necessary to devote almost two hundred pages to describe the complexity of its action in singing. He shows how the vocal cords are stretched and brought into tension to establish pitch; he demonstrates how the breathing muscles should and should not work, and how they co-operate with the stretching of the vocal cords to determine pitch; he explains exactly how the resonance cavities are shaped, and so on. After many highly informative sections have been given over to the anatomical, acoustical and physiological phases of tone production, Dr. Curtis then proceeds to reveal the practical implications of his argument.

The section of Dr. Curtis's book showing the practical application of the material discussed is truly incredible. The voice should be brought 'forward' and 'placed' in the masque. The means suggested for accomplishing this end are simple. Merely commence each vowel with the lips closed, as 'mah,' 'moh,' 'mee,' etc. This immediately transforms the tone quality and presumably readjusts the entire mechanism so that it is brought into a more correct co-ordination. Apparently the vibrations, reinforced by the action of the nasal passages, relieve the vocal cords of all tension and strain, and all subsequent singing is free and effortless.

This concept of the meaning of voice training is, of course, neither in conformity with Bel Canto procedure nor sound reasoning, and literally thousands who have been misled into following this procedure have ended their course of study with less voice than they had before training. Both Jean and Edouard de Reszke, leading exponents of this school, lost their voices prematurely. Melba was so seriously misled by Curtis that she returned to Marchesi to repair the damage done to her voice.

The climax of the Curtis book occurs in the final pages and is a surprise ending right out of Hollywood. The scene is laid in the drawing room of Curtis's home where he has just greeted Jean de Reszke after the latter's return from Europe. Immediately proceeding to a topic in which they were both profoundly interested, the doctor asked the singer what in his mature consideration constituted the most important fundamental of good singing. Solemnly De Reszke replied, 'I find the great question of the singer's art becomes narrower and narrower all the time, until I can truly say now that the great question of singing becomes a question of the nose!'

Apart from the fact that it is physically impossible to direct or 'place' the vibrations set up by the vocal cords 'forward,' or anywhere else, and that fixed, nonadjustable cavities such as the nasal passages, especially as they are lined with heavy folds of mucous membrane, deadening rather than amplifying the tone, make poor resonators, the conclusions of Dr. Curtis and De Reszke deal at best with 'mere appearances,' and not with 'things as they are.'

There are of course, many other debates currently raging whose beginnings may be traced to the laryngologists who sought so diligently to clarify voice-training procedures. The position of the larynx during singing has long been discussed and no one is yet prepared to state with any degree of authority whether this part of the anatomy should remain in a fixed, immovable position at all times, whether a high position is more desirable than a low position, or whether the position should alter with the pitch of the tone being sung. With regard to the movement of the epiglottis there is also general disagreement. Some consider the movement of this part essential to correct tone production, while others, notably Dr. Mills, consider its operation wholly unimportant.

The bulk of the material so far brought under discussion is the history of the earliest efforts of voice specialists to stabilize and rationalize the basic principles of tone production. Most of the preliminary investigations were carried out by doctors who were throat specialists, a few anatomists, and voice teachers with a wider academic background than the average. In many respects their efforts were limited by the total inadequacy of the instruments available to measure and analyze sound. For this reason the vast majority were restricted to viewing the vocal cords through a laryngoscope and studying anatomy by means of cadavers in order to determine the probable function of the vocal organs. Devices for acoustical analysis were of the most primitive kind and hardly suitable for accurate measurement.

With the invention of new forms of mechanical communication during the early part of the twentieth century, however, a far reaching change took place. As the telephone, motion pictures with sound effects, and radio became commercially practical, large sums of money were invested to aid in the development of these media. Corporations such as the Bell Telephone Laboratories, Western Electric Co., Electrical Research Products, Inc., and many others, began an intensive study of the sound characteristics of the human voice. In more recent years these business houses have been joined by a few universities and conservatories whose endowment funds are sufficiently ample to provide the necessary equipment. Outstanding among these have been the University of Iowa, Ohio State University, and the Peabody Conservatory of Music.

The machinery made available to these investigators are, beside the laryngoscope, the laryngo-stroboscope, a device enabling the eye to follow the movements of the throat; the cathode ray oscillograph, which projects an enlarged picture of the exact form of the sound wave; high speed motion pictures of vocal cord action; X-ray techniques used in conjunction with motion pictures; harmonic analyzers of various types, designed to show the number of overtones present in each tone together with their distribution and relative intensities; the acoustic spectrometer, providing tracings of the vibrato; and, finally, the high speed level-recorder showing the changes of intensity that take place within the vibrato cycle.

The general scope of all present-day scientific investigation may be summed up in the work of Carl Seashore of the University of Iowa. With a competent and able staff of assistants, Professor Seashore has conducted innumerable experiments in studying the vibrato, the change in overtone content throughout the vibrato cycle, the effect of the overtone content on quality, the relation of fixed resonators to changing patterns of harmonic distribution, the action of the vocal cords, resonance, and vowel quality.

Other researchers have continued to work from the standpoint of physiology rather than acoustics, and independent studies are still being carried on in an effort to get at the secret of the anatomical function of the vocal organs. The foremost interest of this group is in singing and, therefore, they are desirous of acquiring greater insight into the actual physical operation of the vocal mechanism. Within this field there still exists considerable difference of opinion, although qualified and reputable anatomists now tend to be in general agreement.

From what had once been strictly a matter of opinion the composition of a pure tone is now a well-established fact. Helmholtz has demonstrated that all qualities of tone are due to different admixtures of the fundamental and its overtones, or harmonics, and that when these elements are properly combined and reinforced the final result is a tone of pure, resonant vowel quality. This knowledge, at first glance, provides both teacher and student with a seemingly tangible objective toward which they can work, but this appearance is deceptive.

Agreeing with Helmholtz, Fourier has further proved that identical qualities are always caused by the same pattern of energy distribution within the tone, i.e., the same proportion of overtone content to the fundamental, and with the tonal energy concentrated into frequency bands whose areas of strength and weakness exactly correspond.

With the sound spectrum of a beautiful tone a known quantity, and because certain conditions and arrangements within the vocal organs are indispensable to that quality, the purpose of scientific voice training becomes clearly defined. This purpose is to duplicate specific acoustical conditions previously agreed upon as being desirable. The problem with which the vocal scientist is faced, however, is in imparting this knowledge to his students so that they can sing more effectively.

As soon as an attempt is made to duplicate the arrangements determined upon as representing an ideal tone quality, the question as to whether or not the teacher of singing or his student is helped by having obtained a scientific knowledge of voice production answers itself. *Because it is impossible to reproduce at will any of the harmonic patterns held to be ideal, this knowledge is practically valueless.*

The negative value of scientific knowledge and methods of voice training may be more fully appreciated by supposing that all scientific authorities were in complete agreement, both as to the composition of the perfect tone as well as the anatomical function of the vocal organs producing it, and then trying to apply the principles established toward improving the tone quality of any imperfectly produced tone.

To make this point clear it only becomes necessary to cite a hypothetical case history. This history is of a young student of talent and ability who presents himself to the vocal scientist to learn to improve his vocal technique. Accepted as a pupil, the instructor in the very first lesson shows him a large chart with the front and side views of the larynx and head exposed. The various functions of the anatomical parts may then be explained in a manner similar to the following excerpt from Howard's *The Physiology of Artistic Singing:*

'The contractions of the muscles inside the larynx, including the vocal cords, cannot be brought under direct voluntary control. But these contractions can be regulated by the action of other sets of muscles, viz., those by which the larynx is connected with the skeletal framework of the head, neck and chest. These latter muscles can all be controlled by direct volition. Each of these sets of muscles has its function in tone production. One set pulls the larynx backward, into the position already described, against the backbone. Two other opposed sets hold the larynx firmly in this position, one set pulling downward, the other upward. Finally, and most important in their influence on the action of the vocal cords, a fourth set of muscles comes into play. These tilt the thyroid cartilage forward or backward, and thus bring about a greater or lesser tension of the vocal chords themselves. In this way is regulated the amount of the fleshy mass of the vocal cords exposed to the expiratory blast. Correct tone production results when exactly the necessary degree of strength is exerted by each of these four sets of muscles.' (23).

Fortified with this knowledge the student of scientific voice culture is then shown how these parts may be exercised and strengthened. This is done by striving to raise the soft palate; by adjusting the position of the tongue, jaw and pillars of the fauces, often with the aid of tongue depressors, a specially designed, small instrument which fits under the tongue and which may be used to press the tongue back against the larynx; thyroid manipulations; and by attempting to control the muscles by which the larynx is raised and lowered in the throat, as well as by controlling the muscles by which the chest is raised.

After many lessons have been given over to mastering the function of the four sets of muscles involved in phonation, the attention of the student will be drawn to the sounds he is producing. At this juncture it will be explained to him that a poorly used voice tends to spread rather than concentrate the overtone energy; he will be informed that the vibrato should pulsate close to an average of 6.5 times each second; he will learn that the pattern of overtone content in conjunction with the fundamental determines the ultimate quality of the tone; he will be taught the effect of fixed resonators on overtones, and the nature of resonance. Thus equipped, he is ready to sing. *But* his voice production will not be improved because a knowledge of acoustics and physiology does not make the vocal organs respond more efficiently.

The inherent limitations of scientific methods of voice training may be seen, then, to be of little practical value to either the student or teacher of singing. Continued attempts in the future to obtain a direct control over any isolated part of the complex vocal mechanism can only add to the already long record of successive failures compiled by the scientific voice teacher and inflict a corresponding period of frustration on the unfortunate victims of these misguided procedures. Scientific knowledge of the voice must be recognized for what it is — purely analytical. All creative energies must be directed through a psychological approach similar to that adopted by the early masters of Bel Canto.

CHAPTER XI

'SCIENCE' vs. EARLY TRADITION

The main purpose of this book has been to re-examine those principles of tone production practiced by the founders of Bel Canto. Its secondary purpose has been to show the advantages of the traditional approach over all later systems, and especially to place all scientific knowledge of the voice in its proper perspective. Having fulfilled its primary purpose of reestablishing the first principles of Bel Canto as they were originally understood and taught, it now remains necessary to demonstrate the advantages of those principles over all others.

So much has already been said about the absurdity of the so-called 'precepts' of Bel Canto as they are presently understood, and the absence of any genuine similarity with earlier instruction, that it would be mere redundance to discuss these differences further. Mastery of the art of tone production will be achieved only after these false doctrines have been discarded.

Credit for disclosing the falsity of the doctrines of 'breath control,' 'voice placement,' and 'nasal resonance,' of course, belongs to the scientific investigator. Without exception those who have accurately applied the principles of acoustics to tone production have proven these so-called 'precepts' to be illusions. At the same time, many scientific investigators have fallen into the error of attaching greater importance to their deductions than the circumstances warrant.

In discussing some of the aspects of scientific knowledge pertaining to the function and acoustical properties of the vocal organs it must be re-emphasized that this knowledge is purely analytical. Conditions are shown as they exist, and while the cause of the conditions may be tentatively established, no *practical* help is offered as a corrective measure. Suggestions that may be followed as an act of willful volition by the student are lacking, and there is a complete absence of any real creative force.

The ability to recognize the numerous faults of vocal technique, whether it be with the aid of expensive machinery or by one's sense of hearing, is no great feat in itself. Innumerable sensitive listeners are well acquainted with both the desirable and undesirable qualities of singing and informed listeners continually express their aversion to 'throatiness,' 'breathiness,' 'unsteady tones,' off-pitch singing, and 'nasality.' Recognition of faults, however, does not imply an ability to rectify them.

What has been said of aural recognition of vocal faults also applies to analysis provided by laboratory equipment. After the necessary tests have been made, those familiar with handling the machinery are able to provide every conceivable type of data on the vibrato, the harmonic content, and power level of the voice, and also show how these factors match or depart from established norms. A serious weakness of these findings, unfortunately, is that the norms are arrived at on the basis of the average performance of many average vocalists. This is in itself far from being satisfactory as the norms do not represent a series of perfect tones produced by one or more perfect voices.

A brief résumé of the conclusions arrived at by the vocal scientist will quickly demonstrate the advantages to be gained by using the traditional

Bel Canto approach for voice training. In their studies of the vocal organs and its function as a sound producing mechanism the vocal scientist has sought to (1) reconstruct the anatomical response of the voice parts, and (2) to analyze the acoustical properties of the mechanism.

In reconstructing the anatomical function of the vocal organs attention has been given to the muscular contractions involved in stretching the vocal cords; the effect of breathing upon the vocal cord action; the necessity for raising the uvula for all higher tones of the voice; and toward accounting for the way in which the adjustable cavities of the throat take position when used as selective resonators of the vowel.

From the standpoint of acoustics, comprehensive studies have been made dealing with vowel analysis, resonance, the effect of the harmonic distribution of the fundamental with its overtones upon quality, the effect of the pitch change within the vibrato cycle on that harmonic pattern and a general study of wave forms.

To appreciate fully the limitations inherent in the scientific approach it is important to note that almost without exception every one of the phases of singing brought under examination is beyond the singer's power of voluntary control. Considered from the viewpoint of the practical teacher of voice, all knowledge that cannot be imparted to the student as a direction which he is capable of obeying consciously and as a voluntarily controllable act is largely worthless. Therefore, except for the purpose of rationalizing theories and explaining *why* things are one way and not another, scientific knowledge is valueless for the practical purposes of voice training.

The initial problem in teaching, therefore, remains unchanged, for the main obstacle encountered in training the voice is not in *recognizing* difficulties, but in *overcoming* them. Small satisfaction is gained from knowing that the harmonic distribution for the vowel is incorrect, or that the vibrato is too rapid, or not a vibrato at all; or that the vocal cords vibrate along their full length when only a small portion of the outer rim should be activated. What the student desires to know, and what the teacher is obligated to impart, is how these faulty conditions are to be remedied.

In the field of pure analysis some good undoubtedly has been accomplished by the laboratory technician. Many puzzling problems of cause and effect have been clarified and an important stride made toward an eventual agreement on a suitable nomenclature. Remaining elements of confusion have been seriously intensified, however, by those who have tried to attain a direct control over the causes of tone production without first having considered whether or not those causes are subject to direct control, or without having ascertained the real origin of the cause itself.

The factual data assembled by those who attempt to follow scientific methods of voice training shows in every instance a conviction that the cause of tone production lies within the vocal organs themselves. To a certain extent this is true. Yet, all supporters of scientific doctrines of voice training continually refer to 'the response of the vocal organs,' or use other expressions of like meaning. The question demanding an answer is, of course, 'to what do the vocal organs respond?'

To learn the answer one need only recall that the function of the human body is governed by two processes: (1) instinct and (2) mind. It may be assumed that the majority of those drawn to music in general, and singing in particular, are guided by some instinctive urge. The development of musical talent, therefore, is primarily concerned with cultivating these instincts and, by employing the resources of the mind, to provide the necessary physical outlet for giving outward expression to inward thoughts and feelings. The only possible way of obtaining a satisfactory control over the function of the vocal organs is by controlling the student's mental processes, so that by correct habits of thinking he develops correct habits of doing.

The pre-eminent position of mental impressions over any temporary physical condition is graphically illustrated by those who are genuinely tone deaf and find it impossible to distinguish one pitch from another. In such cases it is absolutely beyond the teacher's power to improve the voice to any appreciable extent *because the student's receptivity is negative.* To the tone deaf, all pitches and qualities sound alike and form at best a series of blurred images. Thus denied access to the student's mind, both teacher and pupil are left without the necessary means of improving the technical condition of the vocal organs.

From the foregoing discussions it becomes clear that three separate approaches have been made in an effort to gain control over the operation of the vocal organs. These may be listed as follows:

1. A psychological approach leading to the discovery of sound principles of tone production and a genuine Bel Canto style of singing.

2. A superficial method followed by those who pretend to teach 'Bel Canto,' but who specialize in 'breath control,' 'voice placement'; who consider singing as 'vocalized breathing,' and who attempt to impart basic principles of tone production by describing experiences of vibratory sensation which are normally associated with good singing, but not the cause of correct tone production.

3. Scientific methods which seek to establish direct control over all phases of vocal technique, including those functions not susceptible to direct control.

The most important path taken in developing the voice is that chosen by the early teachers of Bel Canto. Instructors of that era succeeded in establishing a few basic principles of tone production which were in direct conformity with Nature. Every phase of their instruction was firmly grounded in fact; basic principles were easily understood, and every direction given one that could be voluntarily performed. Progress rested squarely upon the pupil's talent for singing, desire to learn, and ability to work hard. Aptitude counted for more in the beginner than actual ability. In short, the principles of Bel Canto when soundly applied accomplished the primary aim of all systems of vocal instruction and literally 'built' a voice.

The reason for the extraordinary success enjoyed by the early teachers of Bel Canto may be attributed to their sympathy with the psychological elements involved in teaching voice. No thought was ever given to acoustics or anatomy as a basis of tone production. Little or nothing was then known of these sciences, so no effort was made to theorize on their significance to the voice-training process. Quite the contrary, even those principles that were known failed to enlist their interest and seemed to be purposely ignored.

The unconcern of the early teachers of Bel Canto for the physiological aspects of singing was only matched by their interest in the psychological implication involved in voice training. Instinctively they perhaps realized that the quality of tone produced by the singer reflected the condition of the vocal organs. Not being able to directly alter these conditions, they followed the only logical course left open to them and tried to change that which was subject to change. Therefore, the attention of the student was drawn to the *quality of the vowel sounds* he was producing and all subsequent directions given with a *view to changing, i.e., purifying, the vowel quality.*

What might be termed the two basic principles of Bel Canto were doubtless brought to a crystal clearness as a result of a long evolutionary process. The direct simplicity of these fundamentals tends somewhat to obscure their importance, but if we are to ever again have a 'Golden Age of Song' it is imperative that these fundamentals be restored to contemporary instruction at once. To sum up, these fundamental principles are: (1) registration and (2) insistence on tones of pure vowel quality. As Tosi said, 'Let the scholar be obliged to pronounce the words distinctly, or he has not got out of the first lesson.'

To direct the student to produce a tone of pure vowel quality is exceedingly beneficial. In the first place it is a tangible direction, easy to comprehend and easy to carry out. Of equal importance is the fact that this procedure exerts a profound influence on the vocal organs themselves. By changing the vowel quality a corresponding readjustment takes place within the mechanism of the vocal organs. If the changed vowel quality is actually purer, then the new adjustment of the vocal organs will be more favorable and add resonance, freedom and character to the tone produced.

By carrying out this simple procedure throughout all stages of training, it becomes possible to achieve the goal toward which all instruction should be directed, namely, beautiful singing. An additional purpose of real value is served by following this procedure faithfully in that this concept of tone production demands a revised attitude toward quality.

Usually the student who presents himself to a teacher has been informed that he has a voice of 'nice quality.' The mistake invariably made in subsequent training procedure is to *develop that quality*, whereas the proper aim of the instruction should be to *change it*! If the quality of the voice is an accurate barometer of efficiency of the vocal organs, and it is, then an improvement in efficiency *must result in an improvement in voice quality*. As the conditions within the vocal organs undergo a change so, too, must the voice quality undergo a like change. For this reason no attempt must ever be made to predetermine quality, but all energies must be directed instead toward *finding the natural timbre of the voice by means of purifying the vowel quality*. To retain what is imagined to be a 'natural quality' is to hold fast to those limitations of technique which are of necessity in themselves a part of that quality.

Although adherence to the principle of 'purity of intonation' is important to the success of the voice-building process, of even more far reaching benefit is the effect of the proper handling of the registers. The practice of singing pure vowels will always preserve the voice and keep it in fine condition, but it is impossible to transform literally the technique by this means alone. Furthermore, it is only possible to produce pure vowels in that portion of the voice which does not overtax the student's technical capacity. It is absolutely impossible to produce clear, pure tones in the vicinity of the register 'break,' for example, unless an advanced stage of technical development has been reached and the register action nearly co-ordinated. It is for this reason so many singers are obliged to 'cover' the tones in the area of the 'break' belonging to the chest register in order to avoid producing a crude, ugly and 'shouty' quality. Compromises of this kind, however, are unfortunate, for the voice so used will never be able to sing free, ringing high tones, or have a well-produced pianissimo in that area of the voice. These attributes of the skilled vocal technician may only be acquired by having the registers properly balanced and developed.

The work of those who have studied the operation of the vocal organs by means of the laryngoscope offers conclusive evidence of the profound changes often taking place within the vocal mechanism during singing. To some extent these changes are determined by vowel, pitch, and intensity, but to an even greater degree are caused by changing conditions of registration. By developing both registers correctly so that each is brought into equal prominence and made a useful part of the technique, the vocal organs will be trained to respond more efficiently. Thus, it is possible by means of 'purity of intonation' and register development to change every fundamental characteristic of the voice. As a result of this procedure a 'weak voice may become strong' and brought to its fullest development. This development will be reflected in an increase of resonance, breadth of range and flexibility to a degree seemingly not indicated at the outset of training.

The soundness of the early teachers' approach is evident in the fixity of their purpose in striving toward the goal of vowel purity through register development. Experience and instinct alike had demonstrated the wisdom of associating the sounds produced and relating them to a probable physiological cause. These causes were known to be directly controllable by manipulating the registers while producing pure, undistorted vowels. Understood on this basis, the teaching practices leading to a Bel Canto style of singing were a psychological process and distinctly aloof from any attempt to gain a direct management over the muscles involved in phonation.

The inevitable result of any effort on the part of a singer whose voice works imperfectly to set up perfect technical conditions by striving to control anatomical functions and acoustical phenomena by willful volition can only end, as it has always ended, in failure. And this failure has been the experience of all who have ever attempted to learn to sing, or to teach singing, by centering the student's attention on mechanical adjustments of the throat, on 'overtones,' speed of voice movement, or other factors not directly controllable. Let him who would be a successful teacher heed the advice of the mature Garcia who counseled, 'notice Nature's laws and the larynx, palate and the rest will take care of themselves.' This is sound and constructive advice.

Today, more than ever before, there is an abundance of vocal talent eagerly desirous of becoming great artists. Few will achieve this goal. Those who do find a place in the profession are faced with the melancholy prospect of having their careers terminated while they are yet in the prime of life. Just as they are about to become mature artists and bring a wealth of experience and knowledge to enrich their interpretations these performers will be increasingly handicapped because of a steadily deteriorating vocal technique. The fault is not of their own making.

The blame for the vocal insecurity of a majority of those who perform before the public, as well as the failure of many who are brilliantly talented to ever reach that public, is solely due to the type of teaching they have received. False doctrines of tone production are now the rule, rather than the exception, with the result that standards of vocal performance have steadily declined.

In attempting to rectify the sorry plight of the average vocal student it is mandatory for teachers of singing to return to those first principles of tone production practiced so successfully by the teachers of Bel Canto during the seventeenth and eighteenth centuries. There is no reason why, if these principles are intelligently applied, there should not be another great era of virtuoso singing. Virtuoso singing not for the sake of virtuosity itself, but to allow the sensitive artist to give full expression to his inner conviction and understanding of the great masterpieces of music. Mastery over the techniques of Bel Canto singing is the surest guarantee of this achievement.

BIBLIOGRAPHY

1. Bacon, Richard Mackenzie: *Elements of Vocal Science* (London: Baldwin, Cradock & Joy, 1824)

2. Bartholomew, Wilmer T.: *A Survey of Recent Voice Research (Oberlin, Ohio: Proceedings of the Music Teachers National Association, 1937)*

3. Behnke, Emil: *The Mechanism of the Human Voice* (London: *J. Curwen & Sons, 1880)*

4. Brower, Harriette: *Vocal Mastery* (New York: Frederick A. Stokes Co., 1920)

5. Browne, Lennox, and Behnke, Emil: *Voice, Song and Speech* (New York: G. P. Putnam's Sons, 1900)

6. Burney, Charles: *A General History of Music* (London, 1776-89; G. T. Foulis & Co., 1935)

7. Clippinger, David Alva: *The Head Voice and Other Problems* (Boston: Oliver Ditson, 1917; Theodore Presser, Philadelphia, distributors)

8. Curtis, H. Holbrook: *Voice Building and Tone Placing* (New York: D. Appleton & Co., 1900)

9. Dorian, Frederick: *The History of Music in Performance (New York: W. W. Norton & Co., 1942)*

10. Duschnitz, Marco: *Theorie of the Production of Vocal Sounds* (Philadelphia: J. Schuberth & Co., 1870)

11. Edwards, Henry Sutherland: *History of the Opera, from Monteverdi to Donizetti* (London: W. H. Allen & Co., 1862)

12. Ferrari, Giacomo Gotifredo: *A Concise Treatise on Italian Singing* (London: G. Schulze & J. Dean, 1818)

13. Fields, Victor Alexander: *Training the Singing Voice* (New York: King's Crown Press, 1947)

14. Fletcher, Harvey: *Speech and Hearing* (New York: D. Van Nostrand Co., 1929)

15. Garcia, Manuel: *Hints on Singing,* translated by Beata Garcia (London: E. Ascherberg & Co., 1894)

16. Goldschmidt, Hugo: *Die italienische Gesangmethode des XVII Jahrhunderts (Breslau: Silesian Press, 1892)*

17. *Grove's Dictionary of Music and Musicians,* 4th edition (London: The Macmillan Company, 1940)

18. Hallock, William, and Muckey, Floyd S.: *Voice Production and Analysis* (New York: 'Looker-on'Press, 1897)

19. Helmholtz, H. L. F.: *On the Sensations of Tone,* 2nd English Edition (London: Longmans, Green & Co., 1885)

20. Helmore, Frederick: *The Italian Registers* (London: J. Masters 8c Co., 1887)

21. Henderson, W. J.: *The Art of Singing* (New York: The Dial Press, 1938)

22. ————————————: *Early History of Singing* (New York: Longmans, Green & Co., 1921)

23. Howard, John: *The Physiology of Artistic Singing* (Boston, 1886, privately printed)

24. James, William: *The Principles of Psychology* (New York: Henry Holt & Co., 1918)

25. Klein, Herman: *The Golden Age of Opera* (London: G. Routledge & Sons, 1933)

26. Kofler, Leo: *The Art of Breathing as the Basis of Tone- Production ['The Old Italian Method']* (New York: E. S. Werner & Co., 1897)

27. Kwartin, Bernard: *Fundamentals of Vocal Art* (New York, 1941; Omega Music Edition, distributors)

28. Lang, Paul Henry: *Music in Western Civilization* (New York: W. W. Norton & Co., 1941)

29. Lamperti, Francesco: *A Treatise on the Art of Singing,* translated by J. C. Griffith (London: G. Ricordi & Co., 1877[?])

30. Lehmann, Lilli: *How to Sing,* translated by Richard Aldrich, 3rd revised edition (New York: The Macmillan Company, 1941)

31. Lunn, Charles: *The Philosophy of Voice* (London, 1878; New York: G. Schirmer, 1903)

32. Mackenzie, Sir Morell: *The Hygiene of the Vocal Organs* (London, 1888; Belmar, N. J.: E. S. Werner & Co., 1928)

33. Mancini, Giovanni Battista: *Practical Reflections on the Figurative Art of Singing* (Milan, 1776; translated by Pietro Buzzi; Boston: The Gorham Press, 1912)

34. Mannstein, Heinrich F.: *Die grosse italienische Gesangschule* (Dresden, 1834)

35. —————————————: *History of Song* (Leipzig, 1845)

36. Marchesi, Blanche: *The Singer's Catechism and Creed* (London: J. M. Dent & Sons, 1932)

37. Marchesi, Salvatore: *A Vademecum for Singing Teachers and Pupils* (New York: G. Schirmer, 1902)

38. Miller, Dayton C.: *The Science of Musical Sounds* (New York: The Macmillan Company, 1916)

39. Mills, T. Wesley: *An Examination of Some Controverted Points of the Physiology of Voice — Especially the Registers of the Singing Voice and the Falsetto* (Cambridge, 1883, privately printed)

40. ————————————: *Voice Production in Singing and Speaking* (Philadelphia: J. B. Lippincott Co., 1913)

41. Moore, John Weeks: *Encyclopædia of Music* (Boston: J. P. Jewett & Co., 1854)

42. Nathan, Isaac: *Musurgia Vocalis* (London, 1836)

43. Negus, Victor Ewings: *The Mechanism of the Larynx* (St. Louis: C. V. Mosby Co., 1929)

44. Parry, C. Hubert: *The Evolution of the Art of Music* (New York: D. Appleton & Co., 1908)

45. Praetorius, Carl: *The Tone Placed and Developed* (Chicago: Faulkner & Ryan, 1907)

46. Redfield, John: *Music, a Science and an Art* (New York: Alfred A. Knopf, 1928)

47. Scripture, Edward Wheeler: *The New Psychology* (London: W. Scott, 1897)

48. ————————————: *The Study of Speech Curves* (Washington: Carnegie Institute of Washington, Publication No. 44, 1906)

49. Seashore, Carl: *Psychology of Music* (New York: McGraw-Hill Book Co., 1938)

50. Shakespeare, William: *Plain Words on Singing* (New York: G. P. Putnam's Sons, 1924)

51. Stanley, Douglas: *The Science of Voice* (New York: Carl Fischer, Inc., 1929)

52. Stewart, George Walter: *Introductory Acoustics* (New York: D. Van Nostrand Co., 1933)

53. Taylor, David C.: *New Light on the Old Italian Method* (New York: The H. W. Gray Co., 1916)

54. Tenducci, Giusto Ferdinando: *Instructions of Mr. Tenducci, to His Scholars* (London: Longman & Broderip, 1785[?])

55. Tosi, Pietro Francesco: *Observations on the Florid Song* (Bologna, 1723: English translation by Mr. Galliard, 1742; London: Wm. Reeves, 1905, reprint)

56. White, Ernest G.: *Sinus Tone Production* (London: J. M. Dent & Sons, 1938)

57. ————————————: The Voice Beautiful in Speech and Song (London: J. M. Dent & Sons, 1918)

www.ingramcontent.com/pod-product-compliance
Lightning Source LLC
Chambersburg PA
CBHW060532160726
47991CB00001B/295